D1318899

The
JACK RUSSELL TERRIER

EDITED BY
EMILY BATES

BEST of BREED

ACKNOWLEDGEMENTS

The publishers would like to thank the following for help with photography: Hilary Bowden; Gill Alcorn; Lisa Hamilton; Shawn and Vicky Powell; Jo Sollis; Linda Bigland; Cathy-Jo Long (Turning Leaf Jack Russells) and the Jack Russell Terrier Club of America; Adrian Guthrie and the Jack Russell Terrier Club of Great Britain; Marnie Thornton and the Jack Russell Terrier Club of New South Wales; Hearing Dogs for Deaf People; and Pets As Therapy.

Cover photo: © Tracy Morgan Animal Photography (www.animalphotographer.co.uk)
Dog featured is Neelan's Stepping Out To Gone To Ground (Milly), owned by Sam Nixon.

Page 8 © istockphoto.com/Warwick Lister-Kaye; page 30 (top right) © Carol Ann Johnson
page 41 © istockphoto.com/David Chadwick; page 44 © istockphoto.com/Cynoclub
pages 49 and 50 © istockphoto.com/Eric Isselée; page 57 © istockphoto.com/susaro
page 63 © istockphoto.com/Lisa Turay; page 85 © istockphoto.com/Mike Dabell
pages 121, 123, 125 and 126 (middle) © Turning Leaf Jack Russells; pages 124 and 126 (top) © Adrian Guthrie/Jack Russell Terrier Club of Great Britain; page 126 (bottom) Marnie Thornton/Jack Russell Terrier Club of New South Wales.
page 132 © istockphoto.com/Stephanie Horrocks; page 139 © istockphoto.com/Ivan Solis

The British Breed Standard reproduced in Chapter 7 is the copyright of the Kennel Club and published with the club's kind permission. Extracts from the American Breed Standard are reproduced by kind permission of the American Kennel Club.

THE QUESTION OF GENDER
**The 'he' pronoun is used throughout this book instead of the rather impersonal 'it',
but no gender bias is intended.**

First published in 2010 by The Pet Book Publishing Company Limited
PO Box 8, Lydney, Gloucestershire GL15 6YD
Reprinted in 2011.

© 2010 and 2011 Pet Book Publishing Company Limited.

All rights reserved
No part of this book may be reproduced or transmitted in any form or by any means, electronic or mechanical,
including photocopying, recording, or by any information storage and retrieval system,
without permission in writing from the publisher.

ISBN
978-1-906305-25-3
1-906305-25-0

Printed and bound in China through Printworks Int. Ltd.

CONTENTS

GETTING TO KNOW THE JACK RUSSELL TERRIER

Chapter 1

There is no denying the fact that the Jack Russell Terrier was originally bred as a working dog and as such, he is bold and energetic, ever ready to run, chase, hunt and flush out prey. A happy individual, he is also intelligent and assertive. This should always be borne in mind when you take a Jack Russell out with other dogs, for he will be quick to announce that he is the 'boss', however large the other dogs may be! Jack Russells do not always get on well with their own kind, so care must be taken if you plan to keep more than one. This is also true of puppies, who will become assertive at only a few weeks of age unless they are closely supervised.

Although essentially a working dog, the Jack Russell will have just as much fun chasing a toy around the sitting room as hunting a fox, which makes him a great family pet, as long as he is kept active in both mind and body. However, it is important to bear in mind that a Jack Russell bred in a family home, rather than on a working farm, is still more than capable of chasing and killing the odd mouse or rat if it happens to cross his path. Of all the terrier breeds, the Jack Russell is perhaps the one that has remained closest to the purpose for which he was originally bred. This is a dog that adores open spaces, has boundless energy and

MOOD SWINGS

The Jack Russell is known for sudden changes in mood; at one moment he can be happily enjoying a cuddle with you on the sofa, and the very next he can have turned into top-flight hunter, ready to attack a passing fly, a delicately fluttering leaf or, worse still, next-door's cat. This ability to change moods in a split second is not evidence of an unsound temperament; it was a trait that was highly desired by the hunters who created this smart little working terrier, and so dogs of this type were specifically selected and bred from.

7

The Jack Russell is a breed with personality plus.

is capable of running all day – as if he were out with the hounds – even though he may just be making full use of the local park. But it cannot be stressed sufficiently that a Jack Russell must always be under close supervision, especially when in public places, for he is capable of getting into all sorts of mischief!

TEMPERAMENT

The Jack Russell is a small dog but he is big on personality. For this reason, he must never be allowed to get the upper hand or he will be the boss around the house if given even half the

chance. This does not make for a harmonious family life, so your Jack Russell must be taught from the outset that you are the boss, not him.

Always ready to join in the family fun, the Jack Russell is quick to learn and generally responds well to training, provided he is given the right incentive to do so. But a trainer must be patient. A Jack Russell's high intelligence level, coupled with his independent spirit, means he can easily become distracted and is therefore not so easy to train as some of the more placid breeds.

He is also very loving and responds particularly well to the warmth of love his owner bestows on him. Enormously loyal to his owners, he will never fail to protect his family and will go to any lengths to do so. He will announce his presence very vocally to strangers and visitors to the home, but he also has a knack of knowing whether or not they have a love of dogs and will respond accordingly.

When all is said and done, this is a feisty little breed and sometimes his boundless energy can be overwhelming, so the Jack Russell is not necessarily the breed for everyone. Owning a Jack Russell Terrier demands a huge investment in both time and attention. A very sedate lifestyle is not what he needs, though of course there are times when even a Jack Russell enjoys a little peace and quiet, so he must be given his own 'space' when he needs it. This is a breed that thrives on human attention and loves outdoor exercise and activity, but a suitable owner must also accept his hunting nature and be capable of using firm, consistent discipline when required. If not adequately stimulated, the Jack Russell Terrier can easily become destructive, for if left alone to entertain himself, he will probably do just that!

A FAMILY PET

Given the right home and environment, the Jack Russell can make a wonderful family pet and will love the company of children, provided they are well-behaved. He will not tolerate children who might abuse him, even though this might be entirely unintentional. It is essential for owners to teach their children exactly how to treat their little canine friend and to allow him his own space when he is sleeping or resting.

A Jack Russell can be intolerant of other dogs – and he may also show this spirited side of his nature towards people if he is not correctly reared and trained. He may also be territorial, so care needs to be taken when introducing visitors to the home.

Owners say that "a Jack Russell is prepared to meet the world at a moment's notice", which probably speaks volumes about the breed's temperament in just a few short words.

If a Jack Russell is sensibly and carefully introduced to other dogs in the family from the outset, he can become the greatest of friends. However two or more terriers kept together can create havoc, whereas a more sedate dog as a family companion can often provide a more calming influence of this little rogue.

If ground rules are established, a Jack Russell will get on well with children.

This is a lively, intelligent dog that thrives on activities such as agility.

Even though Jack Russells are rarely used for their intended function, being a high-energy breed, they will enjoy taking part in many of the dog sports and this can be great fun both for the dog and the family involved. The Jack Russell is particularly well suited to flyball and agility, providing an opportunity to exercise his intelligent mind and work off some of his energy. The breed's high energy level can at times be frustrating, but will undoubtedly bring an owner great entertainment too! Many owners describe their Jack Russells as "work in progress"! Obedience classes are frequently recommended for Jack Russells, as a means of keeping their exuberant personality and somewhat wayward behaviour under control. This is a big dog in a small package but can be the most wonderful fun, providing his devoted owners with endless hours of fun and amusement in watching his antics.

COAT TYPES

The Jack Russell has three coat types to choose from. Maybe you would prefer a smooth, because you will have to devote less time to the coat, or maybe coat care appeals to you, so you would prefer a rough. Between the two is the broken-coated Jack Russell, so that is the 'happy medium'. The choice is yours.

To be typical, the coat must be weatherproof, with a good undercoat and should be natural in appearance. Sometimes you may come across a Jack Russell with a coat that is soft, woolly or curly; these may be very sweet dogs, but are untypical, for with such coats they could not efficiently carry out the work that was originally intended for this breed.

The typical hard texture of the coat and its natural oils make a Jack Russell easy to care for, so that mud and dirt just fall off the coat when dry. Although more preparation is needed for a show dog, all three coat types actually need little time spent on them by the average pet owner, although more is needed at coat-shedding time.

Due to the various coat types

A rough-coated Jack Russell (right) and his smooth-coated brother.

that can occur, it is often difficult even for an experienced breeder to be certain what type of coat a puppy will turn out to have in adulthood. The only sure thing is that if a smooth is mated to a smooth, all the puppies will also have smooth coats. Because of its polygenic nature coat type can vary within a litter, even with all three coat types appearing. Often a puppy that appears to be broken-coated will develop a rough coat as the months progress, so you cannot always be sure of the coat type your puppy will have when making your selection from the litter. However, a puppy that looks to be smooth when young would be unlikely to turn into a rough coated adult.

COLOURS AND MARKINGS

The Jack Russell is always white, with black, brown or tan; or indeed lemon, which is just a lighter shade of tan with a yellowish cast. The depth of colour of tan markings can vary considerably, even sometimes giving a reddish-brown appearance. Brindle, which is a fine, even mixture of black and light coloured hairs forming a stripe, is incorrect.

Tricoloured markings can also vary in proportion of black to tan and the tan will often develop further as a puppy grows up. Sometimes the black virtually fades away with maturity, leaving nothing more than a sprinkling of black hairs amongst brown, tan or even lemon. When selecting a puppy, if you look closely, you may be able to see a few of these lighter hairs concealed under the darker ones. Looking at the colour of the dam and where possible the sire, will give you a clue as to what eventual colouration you can expect when your puppy grows up.

Again, colour is purely a matter of personal preference and certainly when choosing a puppy there should be many other factors that carry greater importance. But there is no doubting that attractive markings can be very appealing.

Although markings vary, when choosing your puppy you may like to bear in mind that the Reverend Russell, the founder of the breed, liked his dogs to have

The original terriers bred by Parson John Russell were predominantly white so they could be spotted when they were working.

little colour on them so that they were more easily spotted in the field. The white bodies showed up well and the colour on the tail of 'Trump' (the Reverend Russell's first dog) for example, was at the root and no larger than a penny piece. However, it is important for Jack Russell owners today to keep in their minds that this breed was originally bred more for its working ability than for its colour, though colour was important in relation to its

practicality when seeing the dog in the field. Heavily marked Jack Russell puppies are usually sold only as pets.

Ticking, which is a group of coloured hairs against a white background, is often not apparent when a puppy is born, so it can actually look white. The coloured ticking then develops over a period of up to a year, so that eventually small patches of colour can be seen over the entire coat.

Pigmentation is something else

to consider when selecting a puppy. Full pigmentation, which should be black, is undoubtedly desirable, but this can sometimes develop over a period of around one year. Pigmentation around the eye is also not always fully visible in a young puppy and may join up as the puppy gets older. Nonetheless, there is no doubt that full pigmentation enhances the expression and should therefore be considered important, as indeed should dark pigmentation on the lips.

TAILS WIN

In England, the docking of dogs' tails has been banned by law since April 6th 2007, but there are certain exemptions. These exemptions are for certain types of working dog, or on occasions when docking has been performed for medical reasons.

There is also a ban on showing dogs that have been docked after this date if members of the public have paid an entrance fee, but the ban does not apply when a dog is shown only for the purpose of demonstrating its working ability. However, dogs whose tails were docked prior to April 6th 2007, may continue to be shown in conformation events too.

In those cases where a dog is allowed to have its tail docked, specifically working dogs, this must be carried out by a veterinary surgeon and the dog must be no more than five days old when the operation is performed. Before agreeing to do this, the vet must have seen evidence that the dog is likely to work in one of the specified areas. Further information is obtainable from the Office of Public Sector Information.

In Wales the regulations detailing how working dogs are identified and certified differ in certain details. Welsh regulations are obtainable from the Welsh Assembly Government's website.

In Scotland there is a total ban on all non-therapeutic tail docking of dogs, information about which may be found on the Scottish Government's website.

DOCKING EXEMPTIONS

In England any spaniel, terrier, hunt point retrieve breed or their crosses can be docked, so long as the necessary evidence indicating that they are likely to work is produced. The puppy has to be presented with the dam and a statement must be provided by the owner (or the owner's representative) that the dog is intended to work in one of the specified areas. Additional evidence related to the particular type of work the dog will perform is also required. This is detailed in the regulations.

Whether or not a vet agrees to dock a dog's tail is discretionary; there is no legislation obliging a vet to dock an eligible dog's tail. Dogs that have been legally docked will have a certificate issued by a vet; this is required by law and must be signed by the vet in question.

We are now getting used to seeing Jack Russells with tails.

A WORKING TERRIER

The Jack Russell was originally bred to bolt foxes from their dens. The dogs worked alongside huntsmen, who were reliant on the terrier to bolt the fox so that hunting could continue. With this working background behind him, the breed is still very happy to work with people, thriving on companionship. But the fox was not the Jack Russell's only quarry, he could also be used on prey that went to ground, such as the badger. If he did not bolt the quarry, he held it in place until the huntsman dug it out, which involved a great deal of barking, constantly working the quarry.

In Britain, fox hunting has traditionally been a winter sport, so in the summer some terriers were used to hunt otter. Although more recently mink-hound packs have replaced the Otterhounds, still terriers run along with them, bolting the mink so they can be hunted.

Now, of course, hunting laws have changed, so all dog owners must comply with the laws of the country as it currently applies. It is also important to bear in mind that every piece of land in Britain is owned, so it is never possible to take your Jack Russell into the country for sport of any kind, without seeking permission from the landowner. Technically any dog chasing even a rabbit across a field can be construed as hunting, which is illegal, so owners of Jack Russells must be aware of this. It is also important to be aware that these terriers have very strong hunting

This is a hardy breed that is blessed with a good life expectancy – many Jack Russells live well into their teens.

HEALTH AND LIFE SPAN

Although this will be dealt with more fully in another chapter, it is important to keep in mind that the Jack Russell is renowned for its longevity, the typical life span being between 11 and 18 years. This is believed, in part, to be due to the breed's diverse gene pool.

As with most breeds, hereditary problems are not unknown in the Jack Russell and the conditions to watch out for are highlighted in Chapter Eight: Happy and Healthy instincts, so you must keep your dog under control as you will have to take full responsibility for his actions.

The terrier has been selectively bred for work over generations and the natural instinct to hunt is enormously strong. This has led to many pet terriers having gone off hunting alone and having become trapped in earths. Many of these have been rescued, but alas not all, so caution is most strongly advised, for even a pet terrier has an in-born working instinct.

Because he was originally bred to go to ground, there is always the danger that if allowed to roam unattended, a Jack Russell will follow some poor, unsuspecting creature below ground, for he is afraid of nothing. This can be dangerous also for the dog, especially if he has not been trained to earthwork. Several have been known to remain underground in active earth for days, sometimes even weeks, without food or water, for they have an incredibly strong instinct to remain with their quarry.

Because of this background, the Jack Russell can be aggressive towards other small animals, so pets such as cats, gerbils, guinea pigs, birds, rabbits and hamsters should be kept well out of reach if they are to be kept out of harm's way!

REQUIREMENTS OF A WORKING TERRIER

Being the owner of a working terrier brings a great deal of

VERMINHUNTERS

Across the globe, terriers are worked below ground on a variety of game; the red fox and badger are perhaps the most commonly known, but terriers also work groundhogs, known also as woodchucks, raccoons, opossums and nutria, which are also known as copyu. Many consider that working with terriers is not a particularly efficient way of hunting. However, there is much to recommend it as it is a fairly humane method and is selective, making it particularly useful to control nuisance wildlife in farming areas. Use of terriers avoids the danger of wiping out a species over a large area, as can so easily happen by use of poisons and traps. There is also far less chance that an adult will be killed, leaving young left alone in the den unseen. Poisons and traps can also affect animals that are not the intended target, but this is avoided by using terriers for control.

Furthermore, because the terrier does not aim to kill, only to hold or to bolt the quarry, an owner can elect either to dispatch the quarry, or alternatively relocate it to a waste area where it is unlikely to do so much harm.

responsibility, for in essence he is not simply a working terrier by virtue of his breeding alone, but by dint of the fact that he has an owner, or perhaps a keeper, who works him.

A working terrier is also fairly small; he needs to get to the quarry easily so that he arrives at the animal without having exerted himself too much in the process by energetic digging. Like other terriers, the Jack Russell can be no wider than the animal it hunts to allow him to fit into a burrow and to have sufficient room to manoeuvre. A dog that is too large will be unable to get around turns in the tunnels,

necessitating the owner digging to the dog every few feet. It should also be borne in mind that as the tunnel narrows, even a small terrier will invariably have to push the dirt behind him in order to progress further along. This can result in the terrier being 'bottled' by dirt from the rear, in which case smallness of size will be an advantage when it comes to turning around.

Another reason for the importance of a small size is the danger of asphyxiation. When both dog and quarry are underground, it is important that airflow is maintained. If the dog is tightly fitted into the tunnel, it

WORKING TERRIERS

The majority of Jack Russells are pet dogs, but the breed retains strong hunting instincts.

follows that airflow will be restricted. It also goes without saying that a small dog working underground stands less chance of being bitten than a larger dog, because he has room to get out of the way.

Besides being game and having a good nose, another great advantage of the Jack Russell as a working terrier is that it is a highly intelligent breed, allowing it to excel at problem solving, thus enabling it to avoid coming to harm.

Training your Jack Russell to work as a therapy dog is a highly rewarding experience.

RATTERS

Jack Russells are not alone among their terrier cousins in being remarkably good ratters. Most of them take to ratting as if they were born to it. They are particularly useful on farms and smallholdings where rats can do an untold amount of damage to crops, not to mention the disease they can spread.

It is always wise to consider the hygiene aspect very carefully when ratting and prudent to do a little research into the signs of onset of leptospirois, also known as Wiels Disease, both for humans and dogs. Always clean your hands thoroughly after ratting, using antiseptic wipes if fresh water is not available and do not allow children to come into contact with Jack Russells soon after they have been ratting.

Ratting is dangerous for dogs and many are bitten. The bite of a rat can be just as bad as any fox bite and the injured area can become very swollen. Such bites should be cleansed very

thoroughly and if there any eye injuries, or if your dog is having any difficulty breathing, he should see a vet at once.

THERAPY DOGS

Although not every Jack Russell is a suitable candidate for a therapy dog, many of them are. True, this is a very excitable breed but with his good brain he is also very trainable and can be perfectly well behaved when visiting elderly people or making a hospital visit to an ill child.

Dogs have to become registered as therapy dogs, or Pat-Dogs as they are sometimes known. To do this they must pass a temperament test, so if you are interested in this it is good to get your Jack Russell accustomed to meeting new people of all shapes and sizes, including children and the elderly and infirm. Your dog will need to be unafraid of crutches or things like electric

beds, so exposure to these prior to the temperament test will also be helpful.

Pat-Dogs can bring great pleasure to the elderly and infirm, indeed to all those who love animals but are no longer in a position to look after them personally. Such people enjoy their time interacting with a dog, which takes their minds off their problems and it has been recorded on numerous occasions that people's blood pressure decreases when they are actually petting a dog.

Owning a therapy dog is a highly rewarding experience, for it is good to know that your Jack Russell can bring pleasure into the lives of people who have problems, some of whom may have only a little time ahead of them. Just think what giving love to a dog can mean, if only for a short visit, every now and again.

HEARING DOGS

The ever-alert Jack Russell makes a first class assistance dog for those with hearing disabilities.

Badger   **Sidney**

HEARING DOGS

Jack Russells are alert and intelligent little dogs and can make excellent Hearing Dogs for Deaf People. A typical example of how well they can adapt to this is that in January 2009, Sidney was named 'Hearing Dog of the Month' by the charity that trained him. In 2007, as a little pup of only four months, Sidney was taken to the city's stray dog kennels in Southampton where his potential was recognised and Hearing Dogs for Deaf People was contacted. He was thought to be

suitable for training and was matched for a working partnership with Emma Seed, who is profoundly deaf.

Sidney learned to alert Emma to the many household sounds she couldn't hear, such as the doorbell, telephone, alarm clock and smoke alarm, providing her with a great deal of security, as well as companionship and confidence. Before Sidney, she used to sleep with a vibrating alarm clock under her pillow and because she wore her hearing aid 24 hours a day, being scared she

wouldn't hear the smoke alarm at night, Emma suffered a lot of ear infections. When expecting a visitor, she would have to sit in the kitchen to hear the doorbell and phone calls had to be timed so she could sit near the phone.

From the very first night, Emma knew that with Sidney things would never be the same again, for he made a difference to her life straight away. Emma also takes him to work, where after greeting her colleagues each morning, he settles down patiently in his bed.

Sidney has also given Emma the confidence to talk to people in public, for he makes people aware that she is deaf and may not actually hear what they are saying. Emma often thinks of little Sidney's traumatic time walking alone through the streets of Southampton and is so glad he now has a loving home and the life he deserves.

FAMOUS JACK RUSSELLS

The Jack Russell's expressive face and feisty personality have made the breed a popular choice for the TV screen and for cinema. His ability to remain alert at all times coupled with his ability to learn, made him a popular choice in Hollywood. He regularly featured as a hero in children's TV series, especially in the USA.

The Jack Russell 'Razzle' also took part in the BBC children's series 'Johnny Briggs'. 'Eddie' appeared as a clever dog in the sitcom 'Frasier' and of course, it was a Jack Russell that featured in the movie 'My Dog Skip'. The famous movies 'Honey, I Shrunk the Kids', 'Honey, I Blew up the Kid' and 'Honey, I Shrunk the Audience' featured the Szalinski family's dog 'Quark', who was none other than a Jack Russell Terrier.

The list could go on and on, for the Jack Russell has clearly come into his own on the screen and in the UK, Rick Stein's 'Chalky' was perhaps unique in having his own line of merchandise, which included not only tea towels and art prints, but even his own real ale! When he died in 2007, Chalky the terrier earned his very own BBC obituary. A Jack Russell has also featured in the highly acclaimed 'Harry Potter' films.

In America 'Wishbone' is enormously famous, having competed against 100 other dogs to win his role. He too, appears in all sorts of places, such as on bed linen and shirts and has appeared in TV commercials for dog foods, added to which he also has claim to fame in the 'Wishbone' series of books.

Indeed, many a Jack Russell has been used in advertisements, not just on TV, but also in magazines; a bunch of them even made it onto the front cover of the 'Vogue' magazine in Italy. But despite their fame and apparent good behaviour in TV and cinema appearances, owners and potential owners should be aware that such dogs are highly trained and do not necessarily represent the typical Jack Russell personality and its often unruly behaviour. When 'performing' in films and on television, Jack Russells only carry out the required tasks for very short periods of time, so please do not think that the behaviour you witness on screen will be what you can expect from your own Jack Russell.

FAMOUS JACK RUSSELL OWNERS

There are many 'famous names' who have owned Jack Russells, amongst them Prince Charles, The Duchess of Cornwall, Paul McCartney, Goldie Hawn, Mariah Carey, Bette Midler, Serena Williams and Charlotte Church.

THE FIRST JACK RUSSELL TERRIERS

Chapter 2

The Jack Russell Terrier is one of the most versatile of all terriers. He is an excellent worker below ground and provided his mouth is not too hard, he can also be used as a gundog for his good nose enables him to find and retrieve game. It is little wonder that the Jack Russell has been highly prized by huntsmen throughout his history.

BREED ORIGINS

Many terriers, most of which are vermin hunters, originated in Britain. In 1677, Nicholas Cox divided terriers into two 'types':

- the 'short-haired and crooked legged type which would take to earth well'
- 'the long legged, shaggy sort which would hunt above ground but would also enter the earth with much fury'.

It is generally believed that amongst working terriers there are effectively only two roots: coloured dogs that hailed from Britain's north in Scotland, and white dogs from England and Wales. It is from these two basic roots that every type of working terrier is derived.

The working dog from the north was the Fell Terrier from whose gene pool sprang breeds such as the Lakeland and Border Terriers. From the southern areas of Britain came the white fox-working dogs, from which the Jack Russell Terrier arose, as did the Kennel Club recognised breeds of the Smooth and Wire Fox Terriers, the Sealyham and the Parson Russell Terrier. Few of the latter are found at work today, although the Jack Russell is still highly active in the field. There are now even more recent terrier breeds, such as the Plummer Terrier, created by Brian

Plummer in the 1970s and which some might say is a 'new version' of the Jack Russell, although others would doubtless not hold this view.

Of course there are many other terrier breeds not mentioned here, some of them not even bred as true working terriers. Some of them were just small farm dogs, retained primarily to keep down the rat population and to ward off foxes from the farmyard. Others were used as turnspit dogs to turn the spit by working in the wheel by the fireside, whilst some played their part in bolting rabbits from the hedgerows and still others were kept just as pets.

Over time, different terriers were developed to carry out slightly differing tasks, out crossing with other breeds often taking place to achieve the desired result. In the early days, fox hunters tended to use a black

The origins of the Jack Russell lie in the white, fox-working dogs from southern England.

and tan terrier in preference to the Fell or Welsh Terrier whose colouring was rather too similar to that of its quarry. Confusion could inevitably arise when it was not easy to distinguish the terrier from the quarry as it was bolting out of its den. So it was that a more white-bodied dog became desirable, leading to the English Black and Tan Terrier and Old English White Terrier being crossed to achieve a more practical coat colouration. This is the general coat colour now known in the Jack Russell Terrier of today.

THE REVEREND JOHN RUSSELL

The Jack Russell Terrier is probably the most famous of the terrier breeds not recognised by the English Kennel Club. The history of this canny little character we so love, began with Reverend John Russell who was born in December 1795 and lived a long and interesting life of 87 years, dying in 1883. A colourful character, known by the familiar name of 'Jack', he became known as 'the sporting parson' for besides being an ordained minister, he was an enthusiastic hunter and dog breeder. He was not alone in this, for many other gentlemen of the cloth at that time also hunted when not preaching a sermon.

The following is a delightful toast, frequently drunk in ale after an enthusiastic few hours in the hunting field:

*Here's a health to the parson
despising control
Who to better his parish, his health,
    or his soul,
On my honour I think he does each.
Five days in the week follows the fox
    and the hound,
On the sixth, duly goes his parochial
    round,
And on Sunday devoutly can preach.*

John Russell was the son of a clergyman who owned a pack of hounds; his birthplace was Dartmouth, on England's south coast in Devon, but his family moved to Cornwall when he was only 14 months old. Later John returned to Devon where he attended Plympton Grammar School and Blundell's High School.

'Father of the breed' John Russell had a passion for hunting with dogs.

The young John expressed a passion for hunting when still a child and it was at Blundell's that he first had a chance to express this passion. He and a fellow pupil, Richard Bovey, got together a small scratch pack of Foxhounds that they kennelled in a shed behind the smithy, and soon the boys earned a praiseworthy reputation for their sport. But sadly the boys' enthusiasm got them into trouble, for it was not long before the headmaster learned of their exploits, resulting in Bovey being expelled. John Russell was fortunate enough to escape with only a beating, but rumour was rife that it was actually he who had been the instigator.

After leaving Blundell's, John moved on to Exeter College, Oxford having secured a scholarship to the tune of £30 a year, for four years. Russell was not a great academic and during his first two years at university, he appears to have spent little time actually studying. Instead he threw himself heart and soul into the various sporting pursuits offered by the University. He was tall and athletic and became well known for his talents, particularly in the fields of boxing and wrestling. It was during this period that he took up hunting, a sport that developed into a veritable passion.

There were some famous packs of Foxhounds within easy reach of Oxford, so when he had sufficient funds, John Russell had

every opportunity to hunt four or five days a week. But funding was a problem that caused him undoubted trouble throughout his life, and even in those early days funds often ran out; his family, though well connected, were not rich. But Russell had a very plausible story to get himself out of a tight spot; he excused himself by saying that he was prevented from hunting on doctor's orders. He used to say that he had a 'tightness of the chest' and that this was an old complaint. "The doctor won't let me hunt at any price," he used to say.

A CHANCE MEETING
In his last year at Oxford, when out walking John Russell met a

small, white terrier bitch, owned by the milkman. This is thought to have been in 1818. Mr Russell, as he was then, is said to have bought the bitch instantly on a whim, though he did not know if she could actually hunt. He is reported to have said that this dog was such an animal as he had only seen in his dreams. Called 'Trump', she was to become the

Trump – the foundation bitch of the breed. The original painting of this dog hangs in Sandringham.

foundation bitch for a long line of hunting terriers, later to become known as Jack Russells. Decades later, the writer Hugh Dalziel endeavoured to find out more about this milkman and discovered that he was someone who had a good reputation for breeding terriers of that general type. This leads us to believe that there is a chance that the terrier was not purchased on a whim, but was something Russell had actually planned. We shall probably never know the truth of the matter.

Little did Trump, nor indeed the milkman, know how famous they would become, especially by enthusiasts of today's Jack Russell and the Parson Russell Terrier too, for the two breeds are very closely linked. Trump was the cornerstone of a breeding programme which aimed to develop a terrier with high stamina, one that was suitable for

the hunt and also for chasing out foxes that had gone to ground. In order to do this, these terriers needed the necessary drive to pursue the quarry, but they required tempered aggressiveness so they would not cause physical harm to the fox. This, after all, would have effectively ended the chase, which was considered unsporting.

Reverend Davies, a friend and fellow clergyman, described Trump thus:

"In the first place, the colour is white, with a patch of dark tan over each eye and ear while a similar dot, not larger than a penny piece, marks the root of the tail. The coat, which is thick, close and a trifle wiry, is well-calculated to protect the body from wet and cold but has no affinity with the long rough jacket of the Scotch Terrier. The legs are straight as arrows, the feet perfect, the loins and whole frame are indicative of hardiness and endurance, while the

size and height of the animal may be compared to that of a vixen fox."

As Davies said: "It is certain that a good horse or dog cannot be a bad colour, but I prefer a white dog."

Russell was, of course, of the same opinion about his preference for white, and so it is that white is unquestionably the principal colour of the Jack Russell Terrier.

The only picture of Trump known to exist, was painted decades after her death and although the artist had never seen the original dog, Russell described it as "a good likeness". The painting was commissioned by the Prince of Wales who was later to become King George VII, for he came to consider the Rev Jack Russell as a friend. The picture hangs to this day at Sandringham, but although from this image the bitch has been described as measuring 14 inches high, there is nothing in the painting to indicate actual size. It is now thought this height may have been inaccurate and that a more likely size was 12 or 13 inches.

HOUNDS AND TERRIERS
When Russell had been ordained, he became curate at George Nympton in Devon. This was a small parish with about 50 houses and a population of only 240. His income was just £60 per year and this was

CLERGYMAN AND HUNTSMAN

As a hard working parish priest, John Russell was very popular with his parishioners, thanks in part to his cheerful personality, kindly disposition and excellent sense of humour. Often his hunting interfered with his parochial duties, but no-one seemed to mind too much, even when he postponed a child's funeral in order to take part in a hunt. The Bishop, however, took exception to this, but as the child's mother chose not to complain, the matter was laid to rest!

In Russell's opinion, religion was something to be lived each day. He always tried to help those in trouble and to offer charity where he could. At the age of 80, he raised a record sum of money for an Infirmary, having ridden through a terrible thunderstorm to preach a sermon for the cause. Although he often had his own personal financial problems, he was successful at raising funds for various good causes, including the restoration of his church at Swimbridge and the building of a new school in the village.

The long life of Reverend Russell spanned the entire early history of mounted fox hunts in Britain and he organised and rode with some of the very first mounted hunts of this kind. He spent much of his time encouraging people to stop killing the fox, so that its population would increase, leading one to believe that his reason for hunting was rather the sport of the chase, rather than control of the fox.

Often men known as 'earthstoppers' were sent out late at night or in the early hours of the morning to block fox and badger dens, so they would have nowhere to escape underground. Indeed, the parson was also addicted to badger digging, so his terriers had to be up to that job too, and could draw the badger as well as the fox. During the summer months, he took up otter hunting, but fox hunting remained his principal passion.

unfortunately not increased when he also took on the curacy of the parish of nearby South Molton, adding a further 2,700 people to his flock.

In 1826 the Reverend Russell married Penelope Bury whose parents, who lived in Swimbridge, shared Russell's passion for hunting. Soon the happy couple moved to Iddlesleigh, where John took up the considerably less demanding position of becoming his father's curate. This enabled them to put together a new pack of hounds which they later amalgamated with Arthur Harris's pack and their sport covered a very wide stretch of land from Broadbury to Bodmin.

This was undulating land that spanned many large rivers and much of it was wild moorland. This was the type of country for which Reverend Russell bred his terriers. The hounds covered long distances at great speed and the terriers were expected to run with them all day, as well as bolting out the fox when necessary. His terriers needed great stamina and fitness for purpose. At the end of the day the terriers would all trot homeward, but sometimes the Reverend was known to carry a tired or injured terrier across his saddle.

In 1832 the Reverend's professional life took another turn when the parish of Swimbridge and Landkey became vacant. Here there were a total of 1,600 people and although the salary was not great at £180 per year, from which he needed to pay a curate, he was already well-known in the area and this would mean he had his own parish. So he and his wife, whose cousin incidentally was the Dean of Exeter, moved to Tordown, high above the village, approached by a steep, narrow lane. Here they kept no hounds for the first couple of years, but it is believed the Reverend still kept his strain of terriers.

In 1834 he was delighted to receive six-and-a-half couple of hounds presented to him by the Master of the Vine Hunt and soon he won a reputation not only as a skilled breeder of terriers, but also of hounds, their high quality causing them to be welcome in many a pack.

A SPECIAL TYPE

On more than one occasion, Russell was forced to sell his dogs due to financial difficulties, so it is perhaps unlikely that any Jack Russell Terriers today are actually descended from Trump. At the time of his death he had only four terriers, all of them in their declining years.

Although Reverend Russell once said that the difference between his dogs and show dogs could be likened to the difference between wild and cultivated flowers, he was not only involved in breeding his rough-haired, white terriers, once so famous in the West Country. He also judged terriers, but he never showed any of his own dogs for they were bred only with the hunt field in mind. He was conscious that his

Old Jock – a key dog in the development of the Jack Russell Terrier type.

own dogs were different from those in the show ring, saying that 'true terriers' were as different from 'the present show dogs as the wild eglantine differs from a garden rose'. He was also a Founder Member of the Kennel Club, which first met in London in 1873, and he remained a member until his death. A founder member of the Fox Terrier Club, the Reverend Russell also helped formulate the Breed Standard for the Fox Terrier (Smooth), which was then highly popular on the show bench.

Because the West Country was then more isolated than other parts of rural England, the old breed so beloved of Reverend Russell was retained relatively free from the introduction of 'foreign' blood. However, Russell did use the occasional outcross, including on one occasion 'Old Jock', a

particularly well-known Fox Terrier purchased by Mr Murchison for the very considerable sum of £80.

Jock is believed to have been whelped in 1859, bred by Jack Morgan, most probably at Quorn Kennels. Jock's sire and dam were 'huntsman's terriers'. Little is known of the sire, though he was probably also called Jock, but the dam 'Grove Pepper', was white with a slight tan mark on her face. She weighed about 16 lbs and had a 'hunting coat'. It was said that she was a wonder, 'could go the pace and do the trick'.

Perhaps the most accurate description of Old Jock was given by Rawdon Lee, who was a well-known judge and also wrote about dogs. His description, written in 1893, is well worthy of quotation:

"In show form Old Jock was just about 18 lb weight, standing a little high on his legs, which gave him an appearance of freedom in galloping. His colour was white, with a dun or mixed tan mark on one ear, and a black patch on the stern at its root. He was not what one would at the present time call a 'varminty-looking' dog, i.e. one with an unusual appearance of go and fire and gameness in him – he was a little deficient in terrier character. His ribs were well sprung, and his shoulders and neck nicely placed. When in this condition he had the appearance of a rib short; but his hind quarters and loin were strong and in unison with other parts of his formation. To some modern tastes he would appear a little loaded at the

ROYAL CONNECTIONS

Although he was a welcome guest at many of the West Country's great houses of repute, it was Reverend Russell's involvement with Agricultural Societies that led to him being presented to the Prince of Wales in 1865. They did not meet again until 1873 when Russell spent a week in Norfolk at the age of 78 years. Whilst here, the Prince invited him to a ball at Sandringham where the aging terrier man was reputed to have danced until four in the morning, clearly determined to enjoy every minute of this prestigious occasion, even though he had to catch the early morning train back to London.

Indeed the Parson must have made a great impression of the future King Edward VII and also his wife, for he was invited back to Sandringham to spend Christmas week. Russell was very plain speaking, in a quaint Devonian fashion and apparently addressed the Princess as "My Dear", later remembering that his wife had warned him to remember not to use such a familiar term. But his wife's cautionary words also escaped Russell's memory, when he particularly enjoyed a fish dish whilst at Sandringham and sent his plate up for a second helping, whereupon the Prince asked him if he liked fish. Only then did he remember his wife's advice concerning protocol!

shoulders; his forelegs, feet and stoutness of bone were good, and his stifles strong and well turned. His ears were well placed, neither too large nor too small and he had a nice strong jaw."

Thomas Henry Pearce was another well-respected judge of his era and also an owner of terriers bred by John Russell. In fact, it is likely that the very first terrier carrying the Reverend Russell's own breeding to appear in the show ring was Pearce's bitch, 'Venture'. In 1872 he said of Russell's type of terrier, that the wire-haired were the best bred; their shaggy texture did not interfere with the profile of the dog, despite the shaggy eyebrow

and pronounced moustache. The eyebrow, he said, was a great mark and gave the dog a look of a Bristol merchant! Pearce said Russell's terriers had a keen jaw that was narrow, but strong, whilst their limbs were well-set. The back was long and the ears small. White was the prevailing colour, but one of the best terriers bred by him was actually a pale tortoise-shell, mixed with white and grey. This belonged to the notable huntsman, Lord Poltimore and was a hard-coated, enduring dog, fit for any work, however hard. The rough jacket defied all weather.

Reverend Russell's terriers brought the white terrier to the notice of sportsmen and the pluck of the white fox terrier certainly proved to be what was needed in the hunting field. Reverend Russell made it well known that he abhorred the Bulldog cross, considering the blood of the Bulldog to be ideal for rat-pits and badger-baiting, but he thought it detrimental when working with Foxhounds.

END OF AN ERA
Time was moving on and in 1873 Will Rawle, Russell's kennelman of 40 years standing, died, leaving a great gap in his life. By this time his wife's health was also declining, so preventing her from visiting Sandringham with

her husband on that first occasion. After almost 50 years of marriage, Penelope died on New Year's Day 1875.

Life in those closing years must have been very difficult for the Parson, in part because he had made some unwise investments so he was in a poor financial state too. To help him out, Lord Poltimore offered him the living of Black Torrington which was £500 per year instead of the £200 fee he was by then receiving at Swimbridge. From correspondence he sent to his friend Reverend Davies, who by now was retired, we know that he had great misgivings about leaving his parishioners at Swimbridge where he had lived in peace and happiness for half a century; but presumably the financial offer was too good to refuse.

He moved into Black Torrington Rectory in 1879, where he had new stables built for his two hunters and to house the terriers he had that did not live with him in the house. How devastated he must have been when soon afterwards, the buildings were destroyed and all their four-legged inhabitants were killed in the fire which tore it apart. He was understandably lonely and unhappy and in consequence chose to spend much of his time away from home.

Finances though, were in a better state than they had been, so although Russell did not replace his horses following the fire, he did continue to hunt. He

By the time of his death in 1883, Reverend John Russell had been involved with terriers for more than 65 years.

had parted with his pack of Foxhounds in 1871 – they had gone to Henry Villebois, Master of the West Norfolk. But Russell was so miserable without his hounds that he put together a scratch pack of Harriers, which stayed with him until 1882. He once again visited the Prince and Princess of Wales at Sandringham that same year, but by now his health was failing.

By 1883, Reverend John Russell had been involved with terriers for 65 years. For some mysterious reason, in the spring of that year Russell gathered together all his sermons, along with papers he had collected

recording his work with the terriers he so loved. These he spread on the veranda, overlooking the rolling countryside, presumably recounting his memories. Sadly a few hours later, one of his sons returned home to find the papers flying in the breeze, his father having died of natural causes whilst sitting on his veranda. The date was April 28th, 1883.

Over a thousand people from all walks of life packed the little churchyard at Swimbridge to say their last goodbyes and celebrate the long life of the Reverend Russell. And how poignant it was that the Prince and Princess of Wales sent a wreath of cottage-garden flowers, knowing how much he had loved the Devon countryside.

His obituary was published in *The Kennel Gazette*, opening with the words:

"His journey through life may be looked upon as an odd sort of mixture between the old-fashioned parson, the country gentleman, and the courtier… he had a way of his own of reaching the heart that few could equal and no one could surpass".

Certainly the Reverend John Russell will never be forgotten in canine circles.

A SPLIT IN TYPES OF RUSSELL TERRIERS

What may have been the very beginning of a split between what later became known as Parson Russell Terriers and Jack Russells, may have come about when the sister of Reverend Russell's kennelman sold some dogs she described as 'Jack Russells', though these may indeed not have been from the line developed by Reverend Russell himself. It is likely they were shorter legged, working terriers, which were of mixed heritage.

Later, around the turn of the 19th century, a strain of terriers used for badger digging was bred by the Secretary of the Parson Jack Russell Terrier Club. These dogs needed the braveness of character and endurance of the Jack Russell, but were crossed with Bull Terriers to achieve a harder, stronger dog, with shorter legs than the earlier 'type'. To add to the confusion, these were also called 'Jack Russells'.

The next major impact on the Jack Russell came about during the Second World War, by which time much of Britain's population was wrapped up in the war effort, meaning that little time or interest was devoted to fox hunting. As a sporting dog, the Jack Russell was needed less than before, resulting in numbers being drastically reduced.

During the war years little interest was shown in working dogs unless they could be of help, such as dogs that assisted soldiers on the front line or used as ambulance dogs. It was fortunate that because of the Jack Russell's personality and size, the British public, had taken him to their hearts as a pet dog, so the breed was able to make a relatively easy transition from working dog to household pet. But once the war was over, there

NAMING THE BREED

The name 'Jack Russell Terrier' was not used in Russell's day; he simply bred white-bodied fox-working dogs known then as fox terriers. The name 'Jack Russell' came into being after the parson's death as a means of differentiating the small, working terriers from the larger, non-working Fox Terriers that by the turn of the 20th century were dominating the show benches. It was said that the best way to think about Jack Russells was to divide them into two groups, as indeed Russell himself did; one group comprised those that actually worked underground with formidable quarry, the other group comprised all the rest, pets and show dogs alike.

was resurgence in the sport of hunting and also in the Jack Russell's popularity, both in the home and in the field.

In the late 1940s and 1950s some Jack Russell breeders decided they wished to improve the breed further, by use of selective breeding to enhance specific attributes. As a result a Jack Russell arose that was rather shorter and stockier than the one that had been known hitherto; it was also more muscled than those of earlier generations, so the Jack Russell Terrier had become a more compact little dog.

Sometimes though, the working Russells were crossed with other breeds, including the Welsh Corgi, Chihuahua and

other terriers, particularly the Fox Terrier and Staffordshire Bull Terrier. This resulted in a change both in form and function, the inevitable result being that this short-legged terrier became somewhat varied in its conformation. This also led to Jack Russells sometimes being called 'Shortie Jacks' and 'Puddin' Dogs'.

The hunting fraternity had had little interest in showing their dogs in what they effectively considered a beauty contest. But now other Jack Russell owners had joined their ranks, people who had no desire to take their Russells out into the field for work. A few of these people were interested in showcasing the breed, not only at conformation

IN THE MIX

Breeds that were used to create a shorter sturdier terrier.

Chihuahua

Pembroke Corgi

Staffordshire Bull Terrier

Fox Terrier

Despite the activity of animal rights campaigners, the Jack Russell continues to be used as a hunting dog.

shows, but also as a demonstration of their ability to race, retrieve and jump over and through obstacles.

In the late 1960s and early 1970s, various animal rights groups came into their own and protested strongly against not only fox hunting, but also the use of dogs in the hunt. They brought it to public attention that some hunters did not consider that a dog could be useful beyond the age of five years, so many of them put down healthy dogs, purely on account of their age. This caused a public outcry and caused hunting to fall rather 'out of fashion' with some. This resulted in a knock on effect for the Jack Russell Terrier, several

trainers and breeders going out of business. It was now that numbers of Jack Russells had hit an all time low.

Undaunted, many people continued to hunt and the Jack Russell retained its place amongst many of the hunting packs, but now other hobbies had emerged on the canine scene. Although dog shows had once again become very popular following the war years, the majority of Jack Russell owners did not wish their dogs to be graded competitively purely on account of their looks, so most organised events for the breed revolved around field trials and competitions that involved jumping. This cute little breed was once again a great favourite.

The longer-legged Russell was also preserved and in England and became known as the Parson Jack Russell Terrier. The division between breeders interested in working and pet dogs and those who wished to show their dogs leading to a greater division in the breed. Although it is clear that the Jack Russell and Parson Russell are very closely related, with similar roots, the Parson is substantially longer in the leg and longer in head, along with other unique characteristics, including a more subdued personality making this breed rather less self-willed. In 1999 the name of Parson Jack Russell Terrier was changed to Parson Russell Terrier. This form of Russell Terrier had

The Parson Russell Terrier bears a strong resemblance to the original dogs kept by John Russell.

The short-legged Jack Russell is not officially recognised by the Kennel Club in the UK.

been recognised by the English Kennel Club in 1990, during which year it also gained the provisional recognition of the Federation Cynologique Internationale (FCI), a governing body that covers many other countries of the world. Full FCI recognition was achieved for the Parson Russell Terrier in 2001.

THE GREAT DIVIDE
In the last few years there has been a great deal of controversy over the two breeds. In the USA the longer-legged of the two was registered under the name of Jack Russell Terrier, but was changed in 2003 to Parson Russell Terrier. In Britain, the English Kennel Club eventually opened its registry to allow the inclusion of some Jack Russell Terriers under the name of Parson Russell Terriers, which caused nothing less than a furore amongst dedicated breeders. In doing this, the Kennel Club also amended the Breed Standard to include somewhat smaller dogs, saying that because smaller terriers are required for work in certain areas, lower heights are therefore quite acceptable provided that soundness and balance are maintained.

Dogs for which the Kennel Club permitted inclusion, were those registered with certain Jack Russell Terrier clubs, provided that their parents and grandparents were so registered.

Although this may effectively have a delaying effect on the divergence of the two types, many are opposed to the combined registration and will, understandably, continue to breed them as two quite separate breeds.

Despite their differences, both are workmanlike breeds. They are active and agile, and built for speed and endurance. Both breeds have a fairly thick, loose skin, which is suited to their work and in both cases the coat colour is entirely white, or white with tan, lemon or black markings, ideally confined to the head and/or root of tail. Both have a harsh coat texture, which is close and dense, whether it be rough or smooth.

A HISTORY OF THE WORKING TERRIER

The working terrier dates back to 1440, maybe even before, its name being derived from the medieval Latin, *terrarius* and the Latin word for earth, *terra*. In the 18th and 19th centuries, terriers were bred extensively to follow both the red fox and the Eurasian badger to their underground burrows. This was commonly known as 'terrier work' or 'going to ground'. The idea was that the terrier would locate the quarry and then bark and bolt it. The quarry was sometimes bolted to a free area, but often into a net, trap or hold so that it could be captured and killed.

Because of the nature of their work, working terriers could be no wider than the animals they hunted, so chest circumference, known as 'span' is very important. Their chests have always needed to be less than 35 cm (14 ins), so they have the facility of fitting into the burrows, leaving room to manoeuvre. This has resulted in terriers that go to ground weighing considerably less that the fox and badger, which makes them formidable quarry for the diminutive terrier.

From 1750 and for a century onward, numerous 'Enclosure Acts' passed by parliament changed the face of the landscape of rural Britain. Large and often unscrupulous landowners often forced small allotment owners and farmers to sell to the larger landowners. This created many landless and dispossessed people who were bound to try to eek

NO KENNEL CLUB RECOGNITION

Although the Jack Russell, provided its credentials meet the requirement, can be registered under the name of Parson Russell Terrier, the Jack Russell Terrier in its own right is not approved by the English Kennel Club. There are however, other countries in which the breed is recognised by the governing body.

out a living in the cities as a result. Riots broke out and this became a revolution of the rich against the poor, indeed it goes to the very root of much of the anti-hunt feeling experienced in Britain today.

In cities, populated by millions of poor people, many of whom had been forced to move to them having been driven off the land, people were hungry for entertainment and the rat pit provided entertainment. Terriers of many kinds excelled at this and also played an invaluable role in keeping down the vermin in streets and houses. To a certain extent, the squalor of the cities had been created by the very fact that sewage, water and refuse systems were unable to keep up with the pressures of rural-to-urban migration.

Terrier work has been vehemently criticised by some of

Britain's animal welfare groups in recent years and there is no doubting the fact that many a fox and badger has encountered a distressing, and sometimes prolonged death. Occasionally such encounters can also result in the death of the terrier.

There is much criticism that underground fighting between the animals can cause serious injury, but the British National Working Terrier Federation denies strongly that fighting underground is an issue, saying that the role of the terrier is to locate, bark at and flush out the quarry, not to attack them. Hunting below ground with terriers is now largely illegal in Britain; the Hunting Act 2004 outlaws terrier work unless strict conditions are complied with, these designed specifically for gamekeepers and to protect game birds.

A JACK RUSSELL FOR YOUR LIFESTYLE

Chapter 3

Y ou have decided that you want a dog to join the family circle, but there are many factors to consider before making the final decision, not least of which is whether or not a Jack Russell Terrier is truly going to be the right breed to suit your lifestyle. Owning a dog is a tremendous responsibility, for a dog is not something to be taken on at whim and later cast aside. Far too many dogs end up in rescue centres due to the simple fact that their original owners did not give sufficient forethought to whether or not a dog was right for them, not only in the short-term, but also for the duration of a dog's life. A Jack Russell Terrier usually lives eleven years or more, often considerably longer than that, so it is important to be sure that your chosen pet can remain with you for the rest of his long life.

This is a breed that wants to be part of everything that is going on.

THE JACK RUSSELL'S PERSONALITY

A Jack Russell has an abundance of personality; in fact he is 'Mr Personality Plus'! Although every dog within every breed varies to a certain extent in temperament, you can be fairly certain that a Jack Russell will be full of fun, but he can also be very feisty and assertive. You must ask yourself whether you and your family can cope with this type of canine character. This is a dog that has many wonderful traits which will endear you to him; he is happy, bold and energetic. He is also loyal and intelligent – attributes which provide him with great ability as a worker. He is also an excellent companion dog. That is exactly what he needs, companionship and his demands can for some, be overpowering, leading many owners to part company with their Jack Russells, even before they reach maturity.

No dog should be left at home alone all day, least of all a Jack Russell. His brain needs constant stimulation; if left to get bored he can become destructive. That is not to say he cannot be left alone for short periods when properly trained. Yes, you should certainly be able to leave him at home while you do your supermarket

The easy-going Jack Russell gets along well with children as long as mutual respect is established.

shop, but most of the time he will like to be with you and joining in family life to its fullest extent.

A Jack Russell is of course a terrier, so he is always quick off the mark for that is his inborn

instinct. This means that if there are any frail, perhaps elderly members in your family when your dog first joins you, he may be just too bumptious for them to cope with. That is not to say that if a family member gradually becomes more frail and infirm during your Jack Russell's life, that this will become a problem. A sensibly trained dog can usually learn to cope with changing circumstances and will adapt to suit the situation. Also of course, as your Jack Russell gets older he will become just a little more sedate himself, though in general he will remain very active throughout the major part of his life.

JACK RUSSELLS WITH CHILDREN

You must also consider whether the children in your family will be suitable partners for a Jack Russell. He will love their company and will thoroughly enjoy playing with them, but his exuberant personality can cause him to 'play rough' when he gets over-excited. This means that if your children are of the rather boisterous variety, between them they may become difficult to handle! On the other hand, an overly gentle child may just find that a Jack Russell's temperament is rather overwhelming, but perhaps surprisingly he can be very kind and gentle and is usually friendly with small children, provided that the child knows how to handle a terrier.

Jack Russells will not tolerate being mistreated by a child, nor by an adult for that matter. Children are apt to playfully tug at ears and pull tails, which does not go down well. Nor will a Jack Russell usually accept food, toys and bones being taken away from him, unless he has been carefully trained to accept this from a young age. It is important that children learn that a dog must be allowed eat and sleep in peace and to be treated with respect.

Training is of the utmost importance, not only for your dog, but also for your children. Before deciding to buy a Jack Russell, it is sensible to let your children meet some examples of the breed. Obviously visiting the breeder from whom you will potentially buy your puppy will provide a good opportunity to see how the children react. This will not only be beneficial for you, but also for the breeder who must ultimately decide whether or not you will be a suitable owner for a puppy. Another way of coming into contact with Jack Russells is to visit a Terrier Show. These are often held in conjunction with an agricultural show, or may indeed be held in their own right, though in Britain they will not be recognised by the Kennel Club. You are far more likely to come across Terrier Shows if you live in a rural area, rather than in

Introduce some simple training exercises so that your Jack Russell learns to respect all members of the family.

a city, for the dogs that attend are primarily working dogs.

As Jack Russells are not registered with the English Kennel Club, you will not find them at KC licensed shows other than at a Companion Dog Show, where dogs are simply entered on the day. Jack Russell Terriers

may not enter the pedigree classes, but you may well find a sprinkling of them in the variety classes. If you are interested in getting a Parson Russell – the longer legged variety, you will see them at all Kennel Club shows as they are a KC registered breed.

LIVING WITH OTHER PETS

This dog is being surprisingly calm in the presence of a cat – the majority of terriers will chase and are more than capable of causing serious injury.

The Jack Russell has a high opinion of himself and may be assertive with other dogs.

LIVING WITH OTHER ANIMALS

It is a Jack Russell's natural instinct to be aggressive towards small animals, so he cannot be left alone with furry or feathered pets. Reptiles too, should be kept well out of harm's way for this feisty little dog will usually not think twice about tackling a sizeable snake.

A Jack Russell can also be assertive with other dogs, for this is part of their nature, so two or more Jack Russells should never be left together without adult human supervision. Of course, many friendships develop between Jack Russells and other household pets over a period of

time. However, the successful relationships which are sometimes built up, are the result of very careful introduction and management on the part of the owners. For the best chance of success, this should be done while the dog is still very young.

The Jack Russell is frequently called 'a big dog in a little body' and he is usually ready to take on dogs three times his size, without considering the consequences. His particular penchant for picking fights against dogs of the same sex is also well known. However, there are cases when Jack Russells are kept in packs, particularly if they are working dogs. It takes a very competent

handler to manage any pack of dogs successfully and this is certainly not something to be recommended to the newcomer. It is actually the human who has to have the upper hand, so that all the dogs respect him as the ultimate pack leader. In any pack a hierarchical system prevails and the dogs themselves will sort out exactly who is who and their personal ranking in the pack.

If you watch a Jack Russell pack in action when they meet, bearing in mind they will usually not have been kennelled together during the night, you will observe all sorts of greetings going on, including some very submissive behaviour from members lower

THE NOISE FACTOR

The Jack Russell Terrier is certainly not a quiet dog. Remember, he was bred to go underground following a scent; when he found the quarry he was expected to bark either until the quarry bolted, or until the hunter dug down to it. This willingness to bark is one of the breed traits that made the Jack Russell such an admirable hunter.

Not all owners can tolerate a dog that barks. Of course, a Russell can be taught to stop barking upon command, providing he is well trained, but there is no getting away from the fact that he is more vocal than many other breeds. Potential owners should also bear in mind that a dog that barks to excess (which he may do if he is not correctly trained) may not go down too well with the neighbours!

Jack Russells can also howl, especially when kept in packs. This is not something they necessarily do every day, but they may howl for a few days in a row and then stop for days or even weeks at a time. Often their howling also happens at the same sort of time in the day. Personally, I adore the sound of dogs howling but there are other people who do not.

A working terrier barks to signal the presence of quarry – and most Jack Russells tend to be vocal.

down the pecking order. Licking and wide-open mouthing are two important gestures of submissive but affectionate behaviour and even if you only keep one Jack Russell, you may well find that he tries this behaviour out on you from time to time.

A DIGGER AND A HUNTER
A Jack Russell was bred to dig underground – and he will! Not only will he seek out holes in the undergrowth when you are out walking together, he will also often be able to negotiate a way out of your garden, so constant maintenance of the perimeter fencing is a must! It is always a good idea to have some sort of protection below ground too; fencing set in concrete is expensive, but very worthwhile. This is a breed that can forage merrily around your garden for days on end, seemingly without any thought of escape. Then, just as you feel confident that he is free to roam around the garden alone, he decides to disappear off on a hunt.

A Jack Russell usually considers himself 'guardian of the world', so he is very protective of his home, family and territory. Anything that ventures on to it will be hunted off. Bugs and insects make great prey too, as does the odd leaf that just happens to flutter across the garden path. Yes, the Jack Russell is a hunter of the first order!

A Jack Russell will disappear underground at every available opportunity.

THE TELEPATHIC JACK RUSSELL

Many owners of Jack Russell Terriers have no doubt that their dogs are telepathic and this is a trait that is strong in many breeds, in some more than others. Many dogs anticipate what is about to happen and display their pleasure or displeasure of the event in no uncertain terms. I have had dogs of my own who became simply ecstatic in the car about 10 minutes before they arrived at the race track, even though I tested them out by using various completely different routes. Also, there has been many an occasion when I have gone to the front door to open it to what I expect to be the person with whom I share my house, only to find that she doesn't turn up until about 10 minutes later.

TOWN OR COUNTRY?

Although Jack Russells can successfully live in a town, this is really a breed for countryside living. A country life is what they were bred for and their hunting instinct will always remain strong; they need an outlet for their considerable energy and stamina, coupled with constant mental stimulation.

Unless a city dweller has plenty of time to walk his Jack Russell, with regular access to a safe enclosed space in which to exercise freely, his lifestyle will not really suit this breed and so will not make for a happy, healthy dog.

WORK COMMITTMENTS

In ideal circumstances, one member of your family should be at home with your Jack Russell all day, but in today's world, not everything is ideal. Certainly no dog should be left alone all day while the owners are out at work with a typical 'nine to five' job, but it maybe that although the principal bread-winner is out all day, another adult only works a few hours each week, perhaps in the evenings when other people are at home, or in the afternoons, so your dog would only be left alone for a couple of hours each day until the children come home from school. That, of course, is assuming that the children are older and perfectly responsible.

Of course there may be a senior family member living at home who no longer works, which is an ideal set of circumstances, though if you have actually brought the dog into your home, you must always remember that it is you who is

A country home is ideal for this energetic breed that requires plenty of mental stimulation.

the owner and you must not shelve the burden of responsible dog-ownership on to someone else.

When all is said and done, the upshot is that your Jack should not be left alone for long periods, even just occasionally. If so, he will become bored and boredom leads to destructive behaviour. This is not something for which he can be blamed, for it is you, his owner, who actually caused it. The Jack Russell is an aggressive chewer, so given a few hours of boredom he can wreak havoc around the house, causing damage to items that are costly to replace, such as chair legs and soft furnishings.

COUNTING THE COST

A Jack Russell Terrier is not generally expensive to buy, though the price can be higher if it comes from good working stock, or if you are buying a Parson Russell Terrier. However, the actual cost of buying the dog is only the beginning. There will not only be health-associated costs, but also the cost of feeding, collars, leads and beds and also fees for kennelling or dog-sitting if you cannot always take your dog on holiday with you. Even if holidaying in Britain, the majority of hotels and even guest houses now charge an extra fee if a dog is allowed to stay in your room.

Your puppy may already have been vaccinated in full when he joins you, but this depends on his age and in any event he will need booster vaccinations to guard against the most common diseases. You may be one of those people who feel reluctant to give boosters to your dog, but even so he will need some protection. If you opt for the alternative of nosodes, a homoeopathic alternative to the more usual

A Jack Russell may not be expensive to buy, but there is considerable cost involved in owning a dog of any breed.

vaccination programme, this is also costly. Your dog will also need routine preventative treatment against internal and external parasites throughout his life. (For more information, see Chapter Eight: Happy and Healthy).

If you have only one dog, or perhaps two or three, you may decide to take out pet insurance as a means of protection against prohibitive veterinary fees should your dog fall seriously ill. Routine vaccinations and preventative health treatments are never

included under such a system, and in any case there is a substantial element of cost involved. It just means that a monthly payment is easier to budget for and may, perhaps, work out cheaper in the long run, though not necessarily so.

However, another plus point of taking out a canine insurance policy is that many policies offer third-party liability, in the event of your dog causing an accident or damage to another animal, or to property. This can be of especial use to Jack Russell

owners whose neighbours allow their pet rabbits and guinea pigs to roam free in their gardens! Some also cover the cost of kennelling a dog if his owner is taken seriously ill or hospitalised, though not all do, so it is important to consider such insurance policies very carefully and to read all the small print. On an annual basis, a good insurance policy can easily cost even more than the initial cost of your Jack Russell, but if you can afford it, peace of mind is a valuable thing to have.

Bedding, collars, leads and such like need not be overly expensive, but you must also keep in mind that you will need water and feeding bowls and a high quality comb and dog brush to keep your Jack Russell's coat in tip-top condition. If you have a rough-coated Jack Russell and are not able to cope with hand stripping his coat yourself, you may also need to allow a little money for taking him to the grooming parlour a couple of times a year; though this should not really be necessary provided you look after his coat well. However, if your garden is not adequately fenced, you may indeed run up a hefty bill making your garden entirely safe for your dog.

Something else to consider is any cost that may be involved in transporting your dog. Being a small breed, and particularly as this is a highly active one that must be safely contained in the back of your car, a dog crate may well be a sensible purchase. A good quality crate will give you many years of good service and may also be used inside the house if ever there are occasions on which your dog needs to be safely contained. (For more information on buying equipment, see Chapter Four: The New Arrival.)

A Jack Russell is not a large dog, but none the less he has a healthy appetite, particularly if he is well exercised. All dog food costs money, but some methods of feeding are more expensive than others and of course it is essential that your dog has a well-

TRAINING PROGRAMME

Later in this book you will read in depth about training in relation specifically to the Jack Russell, but from the very outset of reaching your decision as to whether or not this is the right breed for you, you should give training some thought and planning. Of course, your puppy will need careful training, much of which will be in and around the home, but as your dog grows older and even when mature, it may be sensible to consider taking him along to some training classes. This usually does not involve spending a fortune, but it is a time commitment as no training will work if not carried out on a regular, methodical basis.

balanced diet. (For more information see Chapter Five: The Best of Care).

TO BREED OR NOT TO BREED?

Although Jack Russells usually make good parents, breeding is not something to be undertaken lightly. The old saying that 'a litter is good for a bitch' is pure myth; a well-cared for bitch can live a long, happy, healthy life without ever having had puppies.

Breeding a litter can be risky, both for the bitch and for the puppies, and breeders are required to follow a strict code of ethics. Brain Auditory Evoked Response (BAER) tests should be undertaken to check for congenital deafness; this is usually done at about six weeks of age. Eye testing is also

important and should be carried out on an annual basis.

No one should breed a litter of puppies unless there are homes ready and waiting for all the puppies. A breeder must also be prepared to take back a puppy or, indeed an adult, if for some reason the new owner cannot keep him. Breeding is a tremendous responsibility and is only something to be undertaken by the most dedicated of owners whose lifestyle allows them to dedicate an enormous amount of time and energy to looking after the bitch and raising the litter.

It also goes without saying, that the choice of sire is something that involves very serious consideration and research; no Jack Russell should be mated to 'the dog down the road', just for the sake of convenience!

You may be tempted to breed a litter of puppies, but this is a huge responsibility which should not be undertaken lightly.

KEEPING CLEAN

Although the Jack Russell Terrier's coat is short, it still needs regular maintenance, so time will have to be set aside at least once each week to give him a quick brush and comb. As a result of their many escapades, coupled with fact that their coat is white, occasional baths are also necessary and a frequent quick 'once over' with a damp cloth to clean dirty feet and legs.

GREAT EXPECTATIONS

When you are choosing a Jack Russell, you need to be clear in your own mind as to what you want from your dog. There are three basic options:

SHOW DOG

In Britain the Jack Russell, because it is not recognised by the Kennel Club, is usually not the choice for a serious show-goer, although certainly a few shows are available and one of the Jack Russell Terrier clubs should be able to point you in the right direction to find out more about these. Indeed, if you fancy a Jack Russell, but also have your sights set on the show scene, you should perhaps consider the breed's close cousin, the Parson Russell Terrier, which is a good little breed to show and not dissimilar in size or character. In Chapter Seven you will be able to read a little more about the Parson, so you will be able to draw comparisons between the two. Another breed worthy of your serious consideration is probably the Fox Terrier, of which, like the Jack and Parson Russells, there are also two coat varieties, wire and smooth.

WORKING DOG

If you want a Jack Russell as a working dog, you would be well advised to buy from someone who has experience of working his own dogs, for he has most probably bred for good working traits and this will be to your future advantage when working your own dog in the field. There are various forms of work to which a good Jack Russell can turn his hand, so even though many sports in which the breed has historically worked in UK are now considered illegal, there are many other uses for which a well-trained Jack Russell can still be suited.

PET DOG

The Jack Russell can also make a great pet, especially for the active family who perhaps enjoys lengthy walks or a good hike around the countryside. If you are particularly agile yourself, or at least you have lots of stamina, you may like to team up with your Jack Russell to take part in some form of organised canine activity, such as Agility or Flyball, if your high-energy pet is not to become bored.

A Jack Russell that receives insufficient exercise can quickly become obese and obesity can lead to all manner of health problems that can considerably shorten his lifespan.

MALE OR FEMALE?

Whether you would prefer to have a dog (male) or bitch (female) will also play an important part in making your decision. Many owners have a personal preference for one sex or the other, so if the breeder tries to sway your opinion, be sure this is not because there are simply no puppies available of the gender you prefer. There are pros and cons involved in either

If you want to show your dog, you may be advised to choose a Parson Russell Terrier which is recognised by the Kennel Club.

sex; bitches will come into season roughly twice each year and this can be a bit of a nuisance, but on the other hand males can have a strong sex drive and can sometimes have a tendency to lift their leg in unwanted places, albeit just to 'make their mark'!

There can be generalised personality differences too. Bitches have a tendency to bond principally with just one member of the family, while dogs often

spread their affections about more liberally. Male Jack Russells have a tendency to mature more quickly than females. It is generally a feeling among owners of working Jack Russells that bitches are rather easier to train than dogs. They are said to be quicker to learn and most say they are more loving and more faithful to their owners.

There is usually a difference in size between the sexes, although a large bitch from one litter may indeed be larger than a small male from another, though usually within the same litter you will find the dogs are larger than bitches. In some uneven litters there can be what is commonly called a 'runt'; one that is smaller than the others, so do not let your sentiment get the better of you, for that puppy may not be so strong and healthy as the others and in any event, it should probably stay with its mother a while longer.

Of course dogs may be neutered and bitches spayed, but I strongly feel that this operation should never be carried out before a bitch has had her first season; then to spay roughly 'between' seasons seems to be best. When bitches have been

With Parson Russell Terriers (pictured), a male (left) is slightly bigger than a female (right), but this is not necessarily the case with the smaller Jack Russell.

spayed they do have a tendency to gain weight more easily than they would otherwise, so you will definitely need to keep careful control over their diet. Although the Jack Russell Terrier is not registered with the English Kennel Club, you may find that dogs and bitches that have been neutered are not eligible for competition in conformation shows, though there can be exceptions if the operation was carried out for valid veterinary reasons and if the exhibitor carries a certificate.

MORE THAN ONE?

When visiting a litter of Jack Russell puppies, you will probably fall in love with all of them! Maybe two of them seem to be great playmates and you feel it would be sad to part them, or maybe there is one that particularly takes your fancy and another on whom you take pity. This might easily lead you to saying you will take home two puppies and the breeder may even agree to allow you to do that. But in most cases this is really not a good idea.

An individual puppy introduced to a household will bond more easily with his new owners than one who goes along with is sibling. Littermates have been raised together and will have learnt to depend on each other through thick and thin. However, as they grow up they may well decide to start squabbling and with Jack Russells this could easily turn into serious bouts of fighting. In the end, you may indeed decide that one of them has to be rehomed, just for the sake of peace in your household. So I would strongly advise against purchasing two puppies from the same litter.

Two Jack Russells often do not get along well as pet companions, whatever their sex. However, there are exceptions; if you have an older Russell who is perhaps rather more laid back than the majority of his kind, you may decide to have another terrier as company for him. If introduced sensibly, the pair may get along well with each other, provided the youngster has been introduced from a very young age, around eight to ten weeks. It may take a little time for the older dog to accept the puppy, but with careful supervision it can work. There needs to be a good age difference between them, the older of the two certainly being beyond the juvenile stage. But if the older Russell is in his last stages of life, perhaps both elderly and infirm, it would really be unfair to introduce a boisterous youngster into the home. Your older companion will almost certainly feel his nose has been put out of joint and may simply not be able to cope with the youngster's antics.

If you do end up with two Jack Russells, you must consider the issue of their sex. This is a breed in which two bitches, as well as

Make sure there is a reasonable age gap if you decide to take on more than one Jack Russell.

two dogs, can be antagonistic towards each other, so maybe the best solution is to have one bitch and one dog. But unless you are in a position to keep them completely apart when the bitch is in season, you will need to have at least one of them neutered.

CHOOSING A BREEDER

There are many avenues you can pursue in your initial hunt for a Jack Russell puppy, but you must not set out with blinkers on. Some breeders are very good and others are very bad, and there is a whole range in between. Thankfully, there are many breeders of Jack Russells who seriously have the breed's welfare at heart, as well as caring for the

dam and the puppies. These breeders will have very carefully selected what they consider to be the right stud dog for their bitch, having carefully studied pedigrees and also the phenotype (outward appearance) of the two dogs they plan to mate together.

Unfortunately there are other people out there who give little or no forethought to the litters they breed, probably just using the most conveniently located stud dog, or the one whose stud fee is the cheapest. This does not bode well for the litter that will eventually be produced and also begs the question of whether a 'breeder' such as this will raise the litter with due care and attention, bearing everything in mind, including high quality feeding and necessary veterinary checks and vaccinations.

Puppies are advertised for sale in all sorts of places and in the present climate even good breeders often need to advertise to be sure of puppy sales. It used to be the case that a highly respected breeder had a waiting list for their puppies, so rarely advertised unless let down at the last minute by a prospective purchaser; but times have changed. I urge you, however, to be extremely careful from whom

You need to find a breeder that produces healthy puppies that are typical of the breed.

WHAT TO LOOK FOR

Whether you have chosen to buy a Jack Russell as a working dog or as a pet, you will expect the litter to have been well raised in a clean environment. The puppies may be bedded down on straw, wood shavings, paper or veterinary bedding, depending to a large extent on whether or not they have been raised in a home or kennel, but whatever the situation the puppies must be spotlessly clean, with fresh, dry bedding. Although I always feel that is preferable to buy a puppy that has been raised in the home, it is understandable that some owners of working dogs keep them outside the house in a kennel situation. If this is the case the kennel should not be too isolated, for if it is, the puppies may not have had sufficient human contact for them to adapt easily to a new environment.

CHOOSING YOUR PUPPY

With luck you will be in a position to choose your puppy, for this breed usually has around eight puppies in each litter. It may be that the breeder is retaining one of the puppies, so one will already be spoken for. Others may also have been reserved, or the litter may have been only a small one, in which case you will have no choice. However, in an ideal world you will be able choose your Jack Russell, or it may be the other way around and a puppy will choose you!

Personality is important and

you buy. You must certainly never purchase a dog from a pet shop, for this means that the vendor has simply passed on their puppies to the pet shop for sale to a third party, maybe even an entire litter. This speaks volumes as to how little the breeder cares for those youngsters, if he or she does not wish even to bother vetting their new owners. It is possible that a Jack Russell Terrier breed club will have a list of members who have litters awaited or already on the ground.

Eventually, if you have done your homework correctly, you will have chosen a breeder who has puppies available; it may even be that you have had to wait a few weeks for the litter to be born and for the puppy you have chosen to be able to leave his dam. No puppy should be

rehomed until it is at least eight weeks old, so if a breeder offers a puppy for sale younger than that, you should think again, for the breeder clearly does not have the puppy's best interests at heart. The wait may seem like an eternity, but it will be time well-spent for there is a great deal you have to think about and to organise.

If you have chosen well, the breeder will have shown you the puppy's mother and also his siblings, unless yours is the last puppy to leave. He or she will also have been able to tell you something about the sire of the litter, although he will probably not be available for you to meet as he may be owned by someone else. Nonetheless, you will hopefully have an opportunity to see a photo of him.

usually even young puppies of just a few weeks of age will indicate to the observant onlooker how they will grow up. A shy, nervous puppy is never to be recommended, but it is also wise to give a wide berth to the puppy who shows an overly assertive nature, for this may be difficult to control in adulthood. Antics that may raise a smile in a tiny puppy can become seriously problematic in the adult. This can be corrected to a certain extent with careful, dedicated training, but too dominant a personality in any dog, not least a terrier, can be cause for concern.

It is essential that the puppies in the litter appear lively and healthy. A Jack Russell Terrier should look pleasantly plump, indicating that it has been well fed, but the abdomen should not be distended as this is usually an indication of worms, though it may be the result of incorrect feeding, or can be a combination of both. The Jack Russell's primary colour is white, so it will be easy to see that the puppy's tummy has a clean, pale pink skin, without any signs of a rash.

Eyes should be bright and sparkling, without any discharge and the nose, though moist indicating good health, should not be runny. Ears should be thoroughly clean inside, with no odour. Sometimes Jack Russells have hind dew claws, in which case they should ideally have been removed by the breeder's vet at just a few days old, for they can be torn, especially if the

terrier is used for work. Removal of dew claws later in life is a much larger operation and is not to be recommended, unless injury necessitates this.

When selecting a puppy you should also ask the breeder to show you his bite so you can be sure it is not incorrect. The Jack Russell should have a 'scissor' bite, where the teeth on the upper jaw closely overlap the teeth on the lower jaw. At this

young age the bite may change, but if the bite is already seriously overshot, or indeed undershot, this does not bode well for the future of this particular youngster. Colour in the Jack Russell should not really be a major issue when selecting your puppy, but all things being equal, markings that appeal to you may just tip the balance, though I stress that this should be only a last consideration.

The breeder will help you to pick a puppy that is most likely to suit your lifestyle.

THE NEW ARRIVAL

When you have very carefully considered all the important factors involved in owning a dog and have come to the decision that the Jack Russell Terrier is the right breed for you, there will be a great deal of planning to do for the arrival of your new puppy.

All puppies are inquisitive, and if you add this to a Jack Russell's mischievous temperament, you have the potential for accident and injury unless your home and garden are entirely dog-proofed.

IN THE HOUSE

When your puppy first comes home, he will not be able to reach up very high, so just make sure you clear all ornaments that he might be able to get at. An adult Jack Russell is not a tall dog, so dangerous and breakable objects located at high levels are generally out of harm's way. However, he can be a good little jumper, so don't leave things dangling off shelves and ledges, or they may not be there when you return to the room after a moment away.

Electric cables should also be kept carefully out of reach. With all the electrical gadgets we use in our offices and homes these days, this is never easy, but a Jack Russell is small enough to get under desks and behind sofas, where cables may be stored out of sight of the human eye, but not your dog's. Admittedly, it is mainly puppies that are chewers, but some older Jack Russells can chew too and if a dog nibbles his way through the outer plastic coating and reaches the wires concealed inside, the results could be disastrous. Make sure you check every wire in the house on a regular basis, so that you can be sure that no crafty little teeth are starting to nibble through the protective coating.

It is not unknown for Jack Russells to chew at things like chair legs and furnishings, not to mention slippers, so sensible training and upbringing from an early age is a very wise move. Other household items I am always cautious about are cottons, needles and pins. I have never had a dog eat cotton thread, but I did once have a Hill Mynah bird who swallowed some, with very dangerous consequences; thankfully he lived to tell the tale. Cleaning chemicals should also be kept safely out of harm's way.

Owners of Jack Russells should also take care that they can not come into contact with anything breakable, especially glass objects. If glass is shattered it can spread everywhere and tiny shards can easily find their way into a dog's pads, sometimes days after the event unless it is cleared up meticulously.

SLEEPING QUARTERS

Before collecting your puppy, you should have designated a place in your home that he will be able to call his own. This may be a little nook in your kitchen where you have made him comfortable sleeping quarters, or perhaps you have set aside an area in your sitting room. Regardless of whether you are using a crate or a dog bed, you need to make sure the sleeping quarters are somewhere that is warm in the winter, cool in the summer and draught free.

IN THE GARDEN

Outside the house, a Jack Russell will love to investigate anything and everything. First and foremost, your garden must be completely secure to prevent any means of escape. A Jack Russell puppy is only small and being the ingenious little character that he is, he will easily be able to nose about and find a way out of your garden if given half the opportunity. Check that all fencing panels are secure; don't just look at them, feel them to be certain they cannot be pushed apart by an inquisitive little nose. An adult Jack Russell can find the tiniest crack in your fencing and work his way through in no time at all, so check all your garden perimeters on a regular basis.

There are also a number of potential hazards to look out for. All puppies love to investigate and to nibble whatever takes their fancy at the time, and if they happen to eat, or even just chew a plant which is toxic to dogs, the consequences can be fatal. At the very least this type of poisoning can cause sickness and diarrhoea, but severe cases can lead to coma and death. Common plants that cause major problems are daffodils (especially the bulbs), castor oil bush (dogs especially like the seeds), cherry laurel, which is a common hedging plant, the laburnum family, lilies, including Lily of the Valley and Philodendron, a common house plant. Others to be aware of are azaleas, foxgloves, some species of ivy, rhubarb and yew. But of course many others are dangerous too, so a little homework before your puppy's arrival can pay dividends.

Look in your garden shed, too. Fertilisers can be lethal, as can the contents of many other

A Jack Russell puppy will investigate – and chew – everything he comes across.

Make sure your garden is 100 per cent safe as a Jack Russell will explore every nook and cranny.

bottles containing useful commodities for plant care and plant growth. Slug pellets are a definite 'no no' for they can be highly dangerous to animals of all kinds, especially when dry, added to which many dogs and other animals like their taste. Always read labels carefully before purchase and think twice before buying chemical products. There are many organic methods of pest control that are much safer and more eco-friendly too.

Last but not least, make sure that your Jack Russell cannot get into a refuse sack or dustbin where he could find himself in all sorts of trouble. A puppy may be too small to attempt this to begin with, but it will not be long before he decides to investigate. Apart from the obvious dangerous items he may come across, there may also be stale food or dangerous foods such as those containing chocolate, which could cause an upset tummy and at very worst, a serious illness. Just for the record, human chocolate can cause cancer in dogs so never ever, feed it to your dog or allow him to steal it.

It is a good idea to designate a specific area of the garden that your Jack Russell will use for toileting. This makes cleaning up easier and it will also aid the house training process (see page 62). Dogs will mark their territory, especially if they have not been neutered, but as a bitch grows to maturity, her urine will stain your lawn, so if you are a keen gardener with pristine lawns, it is preferable to go for a policy of damage limitation.

BUYING EQUIPMENT

CRATE

You will find the purchase of an indoor crate is a worthwhile investment. As Jack Russells vary somewhat in size, it is not possible to be precise about the most suitable size to buy, but a length of 24 inches, width of 18 inches and height of 20 inches may be sufficient. Remember that he should have plenty of space to stand up and to turn around and you will need to buy a size which will be suitable for your Jack Russell when he is full grown.

Although no dog should be confined to a crate for long periods, it can be very useful for your Jack Russell to be trained to use one. It can be used to keep your Jack Russell safe and secure at night time and at times during the day when you need to go out. It can be used when visitors arrive, or when you simply want to get on with the vacuuming unimpeded!

The crate should never be used as a punishment for your dog; it should be a place where he can feel comfortable and at ease, in his own special space. Most dogs that are crate trained will go to rest in their crate of own volition, just because they like it there.

Fresh water should always be made available in a crate. There are several different types of small container available; these hook on to the crate so they cannot be inadvertently knocked over.

When travelling by car, a dog in a crate is much safer than one just sitting the back of the car, or on the seat. If you brake suddenly and another car runs into your own there is no fear that your dog will be jolted forward, probably injuring himself and you too. Also if you are injured and unable to help your dog, anyone approaching your vehicle can hopefully retrieve the dogs without fear of their escape. In a worst case scenario, and it does sometimes

happen, in an accident dogs that are allowed to be free inside the car simply escape and run off in fright, either to be killed on the road or else they never return to their owners.

On the subject of injury, sometimes when a Jack Russell has injured a limb, to encourage rapid healing he will benefit from being confined for a few days at least. If he is already used to a crate, this will be much easier for him to accept. Likewise if he has to stay at the vet for a few hours or even a couple of days or so, the vet will of necessity, have to crate him. Again, if a crate is familiar to him, he will accept this much more readily and it will be a less stressful experience.

BEDDING

The base of the crate will need to be lined with something that is comfortable, clean and practical. Veterinary bedding is the best type to use, under which you can place a good wad of clean

The crate is a safe and secure place which a pup will learn to regard as his own special den.

A dog bed will come in useful as it teaches your pup to settle when he is not in his crate, but do take care that any chewed edges cannot cause damage, especially to the eyes.

newspaper if you wish. The benefit of veterinary bedding is that any liquid that lands on it will soak right through, leaving the upper layer dry.

If a dog is travelling a long distance, for example by plane, veterinary bedding can be rather warm for your dog, in which case shredded newspaper, over which is placed a large folded towel, is more suitable.

DOG BED

In addition to a crate, you may decide to buy a dog bed so your Jack Russell has a cosy place to snooze when the family is gathered in the sitting room. His bed should not be of the wicker variety, for he is likely to nibble this creating sharp edges which might damage his skin or even worse, his eyes. Ideally the bed should be one that can be easily washed or hosed down outside, lined with something both practical and comfortable, such as veterinary bedding. The bed should also be slightly raised from the ground, just a couple of inches, so that it is out if the way of draughts.

BOWLS

Your Jack Russell will need two bowls: one for food and one for water. Fresh water must always be available for him, so the drinking bowl should preferably be close by his bed. He will soon get to know where it is. Stainless steel bowls are usually considered the most hygienic, although some

Your puppy will need to get used to wearing a collar.

people prefer to use a ceramic bowl for water. Plastic bowls are best avoided; they can trap dirt and germs if they become scratched or chewed and being lighter in weight, they are more likely to get tipped over.

COLLAR AND LEAD

Although your puppy will not be able to go out in public places until his course of vaccinations is complete, it is a good idea to get him used to a collar and lead beforehand. You may well need to buy a small, light-weight one for use while he is still a baby and then a larger, more substantial

one when he has grown a little and is being exercised outdoors.

A nylon lead is suitable for a baby puppy, for not only is it lightweight, it is also fairly resistant to those many tiny teeth that will almost undoubtedly want to chew it to pieces. Few puppies take immediately to a collar and lead, so yours will probably both fight against it and want to chew at it, too. This is a habit which you will have to control early in life. You should first of all just attach the collar, only for a few minutes at a time to start with and always keeping your puppy in sight, for he will try to scratch it off and may even panic. After a few days he will have become accustomed to it and you can then attach a lead and start lead training, (For more information, see Chapter Six: Training and Socialisation).

GROOMING EQUIPMENT

To begin with, you do not need to buy a lot of equipment for a Jack Russell, of whatever coat-type, as it is not a heavily coated breed. However, right from the outset you will need to get your dog used to having a brush and comb, so these items you will need to buy straight away. You will also need a supply of old towels for drying him off when he trots into the house with wet feet, or when he has been out in the rain. When your Jack Russell

It is important that your puppy gets used to being groomed from an early age.

BONES AND CHEWS

Around the home your puppy will love to chew things and you may not agree with his choices. Chair legs and shoes seem special favourites. While he is teething he will need to chew, for this is an uncomfortable time for him. There are many suitable chew sticks on the market, with plenty of selection in well-stocked pet shops, but always make certain you are buying something of suitable substance, shape and size. Natural bones can splinter when cooked so they 0should be given raw and under supervision. Rawhide chews can soon be worn down to very small pieces that can too easily be swallowed.

grows his adult coat, there are some essential items you will need in order to keep him in top condition. (For more information, see Chapter Five: The Best of Care).

TOYS
As the owner of a new puppy, you will probably want to buy him loads of toys to play with and he will certainly appreciate this. But do make sure that they are entirely safe, with no easily removable parts. A puppy's teeth are sharp, so check toys on a regular basis and remove them immediately, but discretely, if they are starting to show signs of wear and tear. For example, if your puppy manages to remove the squeaky part of a toy, it can be highly dangerous.

ID
To abide by Britain's legal requirements, every dog must wear a collar with an identification disc, but now microchipping is another valuable means of positively identifying a dog and returning it to its rightful owner. Many Jack Russells are microchipped, something especially useful for this canny little fellow with his adventurous spirit and penchant for exploration, sometimes rather too far afield!

Microchipping has been available in Britain since 1989, since when the number of dogs having taken advantage of the scheme runs into millions. Losing a dog is terribly distressing, both for dog and owners alike, so any means by which they can be reunited quickly has to be a good thing. The sad fact is that fewer than half of the many thousands of dogs that go missing are reunited with their owners.

A microchip is a small electronic device, about the size of a grain of rice. It contains a special number that can be read by a scanner, working by means of radio wave frequency. The chip is inserted under the skin, between the shoulder blades, using a needle. No anaesthetic is needed and the procedure rarely causes any greater discomfort than a standard vaccination.

The chip stays in place because the tissue surrounding it attaches itself to the microchip. This may sound a little worrying to the uninitiated, but it is made of the same bio-compatible material that is used in human pacemakers. Of course everything is sterilised before use, so that the body does not reject the chip.

To read the microchip, a scanner is passed over the dog's body allowing the number to be read and through this, if the dog has been chipped, he can be returned to his owner quickly and easily. Microchipping can be carried out at a veterinary surgery, or by many animal welfare authorities and even local authorities.

It is a legal requirement for dogs to have some form of ID.

FINDING A VET

There may be several veterinary practices in your area, but if you do not already have one that you use with another pet, you should take local advice of which one would be best. You will clearly need one that is relatively near in case you have to rush your Jack Russell to the vet in an emergency; but that is not the only consideration. If you live in a rural area, some vets have more experience in dealing with larger farm animals than they do dogs. A 'small animal vet' is likely to have a lot more experience in dealing with small dogs like Jack Russells.

There may be a trusted neighbour who can point you in the right direction, or you could make enquires at you local training class where there are sure to be plenty of people with experience of the vets in your area.

At last the big day arrives and it is time to collect your puppy.

COLLECTING YOUR NEW PUPPY

You may have had the opportunity to visit the litter before the puppies are ready to leave their mother, for many breeders allow potential purchasers to view a litter at five or six weeks. This is always a good idea, but do please remember that when viewing puppies at this young age they will have no protection from disease as they will not then have had any vaccinations. So please do not touch the puppies unless you are invited to do so and after having disinfected your hands thoroughly.

If you have visited before and have decided to buy, you will doubtless fix an appointment to visit again to collect your puppy a few weeks later, usually when the puppy is between eight and ten weeks old. Meanwhile you will have plenty of things to prepare to keep your mind occupied! Even if your first visit is when the puppies are old enough to leave, if you don't have everything ready and prepared at home, it would be only sensible to allow yourself a few days before collecting the puppy.

When going to collect your puppy it is best not to travel alone; if you are travelling by car it is wise to have someone with you, either as the driver, or as the person to hold the puppy and take care of him during the journey. It is unlikely that he will have been in a car before, except perhaps for a short journey to the vet, so he will need lots of reassurance as he will be away from his mother and littermates for the first time and will be entirely unfamiliar with his surroundings. Personally I never like a puppy to make his first journey in a travelling crate unless there is no option; crate training is something they can be introduced to a little later. There is also the chance that your new puppy may suffer from travel sickness, although he may well grow out of this very quickly, so remember to go armed with a good supply of kitchen towelling, just in case!

THE PAPERWORK

When you finally take your leave of the breeder, you should be armed not only with your precious puppy, but also with paperwork and information for the future. If you are buying a Parson Russell Terrier, which is a Kennel Club registered breed, you will be supplied with the KC paperwork registering the litter and a form for the transfer of ownership, as well as a pedigree. If you are buying a non-KC registered Jack Russell Terrier you will not have KC papers, but you should be given a pedigree and hopefully, documentation proving that your puppy has been registered with one of the breed societies.

Depending on the age at which your puppy leaves home, he may or may not have begun his vaccination programme. It is essential that you clearly understand the position on this and that if the first vaccination has been given, you are given veterinary documentation to prove this. This will detail not only the date of vaccination but also the type of vaccine used; this you will pass on to your own vet for completion of the course. Until the initial vaccination course is complete, your Jack Russell puppy will not be able to mix and mingle freely with other dogs, nor be exercised in areas which may have been visited by others.

Another health issue about which you must be well informed, is his worming programme. The most common form of worm found in puppies is roundworm, which is picked up from the mother both across the placenta and in her milk, so virtually all puppies will be infested. By the time your puppy leaves home there should be no evidence of worms at all, provided the breeder has carried

The breeder will have already started a worming programme, which you will need to continue.

out a carefully considered worming programme. You will need to know exactly when the next treatment is to be given. The dosage will depend on the puppy's weight at the time the treatment is due and it is wise to get suitable, high quality tablets from your vet, rather than to purchase them over the counter at a pet store.

To know your Jack Russell's feeding programme is also essential, not only the timing of

his feeds, but what kind of food has been given. Both of these you will be able to adjust as time goes on, but for the first few days and weeks things must continue as far as possible as before, with changes being made gradually over a period of time.

A responsible breeder will give you a printed diet sheet explaining everything, including timings; the least you must expect is a clear verbal explanation. As your puppy

Arriving in a new home is a daunting experience for a puppy.

HOMEWARD BOUND

Hopefully your puppy will have a comfortable journey home and remember that even if you have a long journey ahead, unless his course of vaccinations is complete, which is unlikely unless he is older, he will not be able to relieve himself on a grass verge or field along the route. If you have a hatchback or estate car, you can probably get around this by taking with you a thick wad of clean newspaper, which you can place in the back of the car to give him a chance to go to the toilet if he needs to. He may not use it, but at least you will have a clear conscience in that you will have done all in your power to offer him the opportunity.

ARRIVING HOME

Even if your Jack Russell puppy is fairly quiet and calm on the journey back, going into your home will be a 'first experience' for him, so do not expect him to immediately be full of fun. It is sure to take him a little time to adapt; some puppies take longer than others. He will probably be rather reserved at first and may well seem substantially more shy and nervous than he was at his breeder's home, where his environment was entirely familiar to him. Give him time. Don't push him too hard, but speak to him gently, with words of encouragement. Certainly don't have extended family and friends waiting to greet him upon his arrival, the last thing he will want is a 'welcome home party'!

matures, his feeds will be reduced in number; you and he will adjust to this together. If you do not have food in stock of the exact type and make used by the breeder, hopefully she will give you a little to tide you over, for your puppy's stomach will not be able to cope with an abrupt change as this will give him loose motions. If the brand the breeder feeds is easily available in shops and supermarkets, this will not present too much of a problem as you should be able to find it easily, but if it is one of the less popular or more specialised feeds you will have more difficulty locating it. In the latter case, you will need to gradually mix in the new brand with the old, changing the diet over a period of a few days.

Firstly, he must be allowed to get used to you and your immediate family; that will be quite enough for him to cope with for the first couple of days or so.

If there are other family pets, these too should be introduced carefully and under close supervision. Another dog around the house may well give your puppy an immediate boost of confidence, but then again you cannot be sure how your own dog will react to the newcomer, who may treat him initially as an intruder. Just be sensible about the introduction and things will settle down amicably in time. If you have a smaller pet that a Jack Russell is likely to chase and possibly kill, again it is wise to let him see the small pet, but from a safe distance, the little one preferably caged where he is out of harm's way.

INTRODUCING THE CRATE

Crate training with a puppy needs to be started early in the day, so that he has become accustomed to the routine by bedtime. Make sure you put something interesting or enticing inside the crate before your puppy goes in; it may be a little doggy treat, or just a toy that will capture his attention. To begin with, don't close the door of the crate, just let him wander in and out at will, which he will do if there is some tasty treat inside. If he has nodded off after a playing session, it maybe possible to lift him up gently and place him into the crate, maybe even

leaving the door open so that he doesn't panic when he wakes. Soon enough he will learn to think of his crate as his own personal 'safety zone', much as a wild dog would his den.

During initial crate training, always stay with your puppy, or remain close by so you can keep a careful eye on him, for he may scrape at the bars and attempt to chew his way out. Make sure he always has a comfortable blanket or piece of veterinary bedding, a safe toy and access to water inside the crate. Water containers can be purchased to fit the sides of the crate, so there is no spillage.

When newly introduced to his crate, a puppy should only be expected to stay in for a few minutes at a time, gradually building up; though neither a

puppy nor an adult dog should ever be left inside a crate for too long at one stretch. Night-time is different, for whilst the dog is sound asleep he will have little conception of time.

If your puppy is young and you feel he may still have an accident during the night, below his bedding put a wad of clean newspaper to absorb any moisture. If you have chosen to let your Jack Russell sleep in a crate at night-time, bed him down as late as possible and get him up bright and early in the morning. Give him an immediate opportunity to visit the garden in order to relieve himself. All dogs essentially like to sleep in clean quarters, so he will learn not to dirty his crate once he is old enough to sleep through the night.

Take time introducing your puppy to his crate.

Some puppies lose their appetite when they are settling in – but Jack Russells are rarely faddy feeders.

MEALTIMES

Mealtimes should always be supervised, so that you know exactly how much your puppy is eating before feeling full. He must always be allowed to concentrate on his food, so try never to distract him, though in the early stages you may find you need to give him a little encouragement to eat. Any uneaten food should be removed and disposed of when he has eaten his fill and it goes without saying that all feeding utensils must be thoroughly clean before use.

Do not worry unduly if your new puppy eats very little during his first 24 hours with you. This is quite normal in that very early 'settling in' stage. When his tummy is empty, he should soon eat with relish!

THE FIRST NIGHT

The safest place for your Jack Russell puppy to sleep overnight is in his crate. Understandably he will feel very strange on his first night in a new home and he may decide to bark to let you know he would rather be with you than in his crate. Indeed you will be very lucky if you have a Jack Russell that gives you a peaceful first night's sleep! Obviously you will want to reassure your puppy that he is quite safe in his crate, but he should not learn that every time he barks he will be let out to roam free. If you allow this to happen he will come to associate barking with 'getting his own way'. It will help if he has something he can cuddle up against, such as a safe cuddly

toy, for he will not have the comfort of his siblings around him. A clock with a loud tick located in the room will also be comforting for him.

If your puppy's crate is large enough, you may wish to have an area of just paper without bedding, so that while still unable to go through the night without relieving himself he can use the paper instead of his sleeping area.

HOUSE TRAINING

When you get your new puppy he may still be on three feeds each day, but depending on his age he may already have been reduced to two, or in any event this will happen soon. A puppy needs to relieve himself many times a day and in part, these visits will be tied in with his feeding schedule and daily schedule.

Immediately he wakes he needs to go; he cannot wait – it's urgent! When he is small he will need to pass urine absolutely every time he wakes up, so be sure to put him out in the garden the minute he wakes. He won't have time to wait until you get dressed, so before you disturb him by making a noise, make sure you have your slippers and gown on. Your ablutions will just have to wait until later!

Stay with him and as soon as he has done his toilet give him plenty of praise, so he knows that what he's done has pleased you. You can use a word of encouragement if you like, which he will associate with his toilet; this can come in very useful later in life, especially if you are travelling with him or if he is at a conformation show, for it is always better if you can be sure he has been to the toilet before he enters the judging ring.

When your puppy has eaten, he also needs to go outside soon afterwards and even when he has just had a long drink. He will also need to go out after play sessions; as a rule of thumb, he will need to go out every two hours throughout the day. Always take him to the toileting area you have allocated in your garden; the very fact that he has been before in that place will encourage him to go again. When he has done his business, always be sure to clean up immediately.

Take your puppy out at regular intervals and he will soon learn what is required.

If you catch him in the act of going to the toilet in the wrong place, such as inside the house on your best carpet, distract his attention immediately, which may have the effect of stopping him in the act. If he does stop, and only if he does, give him praise for this and take him outside straight away to go to the toilet in the proper place. You will have to be very careful not to confuse him though, for if you praise him before he has stopped doing his toilet in the wrong place, he will think you are happy about this and will do it again. Your timing must be just right.

HANDLING

Your puppy needs to get used to being handled from an early age. This will help with grooming sessions and it will also stand you in good stead when you need to visit the vet, for it is always easier for a vet to examine a well-behaved dog.

Start by running a comb gently through your puppy's coat. Open his mouth to check his teeth and

HANDLING A PUPPY

A puppy should be accustomed to all over handling so that he is happy to be groomed and undergo routine care procedures.

Pick up each of the front feet.

Move round and pick up each of the back feet.

Run your hand along the back to the tip of the tail, gently restraining the pup if necessary.

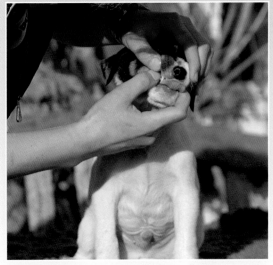

Open the lips and check the teeth and gums.

HOUSE RULES

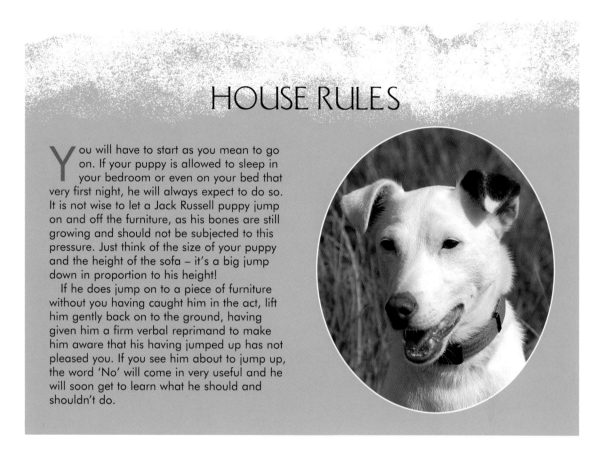

You will have to start as you mean to go on. If your puppy is allowed to sleep in your bedroom or even on your bed that very first night, he will always expect to do so. It is not wise to let a Jack Russell puppy jump on and off the furniture, as his bones are still growing and should not be subjected to this pressure. Just think of the size of your puppy and the height of the sofa – it's a big jump down in proportion to his height!

If he does jump on to a piece of furniture without you having caught him in the act, lift him gently back on to the ground, having given him a firm verbal reprimand to make him aware that his having jumped up has not pleased you. If you see him about to jump up, the word 'No' will come in very useful and he will soon get to learn what he should and shouldn't do.

also pick up his feet to examine his pads. If you have a male, train him to tolerate having you gently check his testicles; this will be especially useful if you plan to show him as this is part of a judge's routine examination.

EXERCISE FOR YOUR PUPPY

Until your puppy's course of vaccinations is complete, he will not be able to go out in public places, nor should strange dogs be allowed to visit your house for they may themselves have been in contact with disease, against which he will have no immunity. But Jack Russell puppies have an enormous amount of energy and this will have to be released, either in your garden or around your home if there is sufficient space for a good game in a safe area.

The principal reason for Jack Russell Terriers becoming unruly and destructive is that they are not given sufficient opportunity to exercise their minds and bodies. They must have an outlet to burn off all their excess energy. They will however, need someone to play with, for if left alone they will probably just create mischief and mischief can be dangerous. There are lots of games in which you can interact with your puppy, such as ball games and playing games with safe toys.

Don't encourage your puppy to exercise too much when the weather is particularly hot. A strenuous ball game at lunchtime in the hot summer months is not at all a good idea. Nor should you play running games with a young puppy. Although this is a small breed, his bones are still

A Jack Russell thrives on exercise, but do not allow your puppy to do too much while he is still growing.

growing so should not have undue stress placed upon them until he is more mature. A puppy must be allowed to rest as frequently as he wishes, so when he shows signs of tiredness don't force him to carry on playing. All puppies need an enormous amount of rest. Remember never to let him take part in strenuous exercise after his food or he will risk getting bloat, which is a life threatening condition. He will

need to go out to relieve himself certainly, but allow a further hour before major games are allowed.

TAKING ON A RESCUED DOG

An alternative to purchasing a young puppy is to take a rescued Jack Russell, or sometimes breeders wish to find new homes for bitches that have whelped litters and have been retired from breeding. There are undoubtedly pros and cons.

In taking on an older dog, the exuberance of puppyhood will be past, so you will have a more mature dog to join your household, which may perhaps, be substantially less bubbly and boisterous. On the other hand, you will have missed out on the many months of pleasure a puppy will give you, watching his antics and joining in his games.

You cannot necessarily expect that an older dog will come to

You will need time and patience to help an older dog to settle into a new home.

you ready house-trained. Even if he has been trained with his former owner, his new environment will take some getting used to and he will have to learn the house rules afresh. If he has been kenneled, which applies to some of the dogs that end up in rescue as well as to some breeding bitches, the dog may never he have been house-trained at all. It will undoubtedly be more difficult to train an older dog, as he will already have become set in his ways.

Then there is the question of temperament. Many a rescued or re-homed dog can be a wonderful companion, thoroughly appreciating the new attention he is receiving, albeit a little late in life. However, there are other cases where a Jack Russell has ended up in rescue because his temperament is not good; this may not be the dog's fault, it could very easily be that of an owner who has mistreated

their dog. Often a terrier will readjust and become a very contented companion, returning all the love he is being given by his new found friend. But unfortunately, this is not always the case. It is therefore important that you find out as much as you can about an adult dog's background and if you have any doubts you should look elsewhere, especially if you have small children and their welfare to consider.

THE BEST OF CARE

Chapter

5

The Jack Russell Terrier is a small dog with a durable coat, so he is not particularly challenging to look after – the challenge comes primarily in coping with his lively mind and temperament! In addition, this breed does not have a history of too many health issues so this aspect usually presents few problems too, although there can of course be exceptions.

Your Jack Russell's coat will not require constant, tedious grooming, but it will need attention. Always remember that a healthy coat is developed both from inside and out. Correct feeding will play a very large part in keeping your Jack Russell healthy in both body and coat. In addition to diet and coat care, exercise is also top priority as your aim is to keep your Jack Russell fit and in the peak of good health.

DIET AND NUTRITION
What you feed your dog will play a very important part in his ultimate health and wellbeing. As your puppy has matured into adulthood, you will slowly have changed his diet to one that suits him and your own lifestyle. Some people feed only one meal each day; if so this is usually in the late afternoon or early evening, never too late in the day or he won't have had the chance to fully digest it before settling down for the night. Those who feed just one meal a day, often give a small snack at the other end of the day. Others like to feed two smaller meals each day, but in both cases the overall intake of food should be about the same; two meals a day does not mean two large ones!

There are many, many options as to what you actually feed your dog, increasingly so with the enormous variety of ready prepared foods available in the shops, not only in pet stores but in supermarkets too. The choice is endless. Although dogs are basically carnivores, they can actually benefit from eating plant materials too, so essentially they are omnivorous. Some people who are vegetarians themselves also feed a vegetarian diet to their dogs, though this something I personally would not do, despite having been vegetarian for a large part of my own life.

A JACK RUSSELL'S NEEDS
The aim is to feed a well balanced diet that will cater for all your dog's nutritional needs. The Jack Russell is a highly active breed, so he will require slightly higher protein content than a more sedentary dog that just spends his life lazing by the fireside. A working terrier is likely to need a higher protein content than one that is kept purely as a

FEEDING DURING THE GROWTH PERIOD

While your Jack Russell is growing he will have a greater need for energy, protein, vitamins and minerals than does a fully-grown, adult dog. If you bear in mind that a puppy's birth weight usually roughly doubles in the first seven to ten days, this will give you an idea of how important this is. By four months of age, a Jack Russell puppy will normally weigh about half of his eventual adult weight.

pet or as a show dog and an obese dog, or one with a tendency to become obese, is usually best kept on a low-protein diet.

It is generally accepted that a small terrier needs about 65 kcal per kilogram of body weight, which equals roughly 30 kcal per lb of body weight. If you feed your dog a pre-prepared food, you should find all details of content on the side or back of the tin or packet. Sometimes the actual calories are not given, but if you feed food from a reputable company, this information should be provided to you upon request.

Nervous dogs, or those that are particularly prone to stress, do not actually need higher protein content than most other dogs. They simply require a higher calorific intake. However, if the energy intake is too high, this will result in obesity.

CHOOSING A DIET

PREPARED FOOD

When feeding a diet prepared by a manufacturer, you have to be very careful not to unbalance an otherwise well-balanced diet. Certainly as humans we would not wish to eat the same food day in and day out, but dogs do not necessarily think along those lines, just so long as they feel well fed and well nourished. Although I feed high quality dried food myself, I do add just a little 'something' for variety's sake each day; this may be a very small portion of fresh meat

The aim is to feed your dog a well balanced diet that is suited to his age and lifestyle.

CHOOSING A DIET

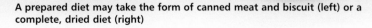

A prepared diet may take the form of canned meat and biscuit (left) or a complete, dried diet (right)

If you are feeding a fresh, homemade diet, you will need to make sure it has all the nutrients your dog requires.

or tinned food or even a few fresh vegetables. However, I regularly check my dogs' weight and I know them well enough to notice if any change in diet has caused them to become a fraction more hyperactive than usual, or if they have loose motions, something a change in diet can easily cause.

HOMEMADE DIET

With today's hectic lifestyle, most owners find it much easier and more convenient to feed a ready prepared food that can simply be purchased over the counter, but there are people who still like to feed a freshly prepared diet. This is certainly possible, but it is less likely that the diet will be so accurately balanced for a canine as one scientifically prepared by a good manufacturer. I stress the word 'good', for the quality of pre-

prepared foods can vary considerably, just as they vary greatly in cost.

Many different foods can be used in a canine meal prepared by a dog's owner: fruit, vegetables, eggs, rice and of course both red and white meats. However, if feeding such a diet, it is usually wise to also give your dog vitamin and mineral supplements, which are not generally needed otherwise.

BARF DIET

Some owners successfully feed the BARF diet, the name of which stands for Bones And Raw Food, or some say Biologically Appropriate Raw Food. Basically it just means that dogs are fed the way that nature intended. It is true that in the wild dogs lived off whole carcasses; this included not only the meat, skin and internal

organs, but also the contents of the stomach, which usually contained digested vegetation incorporating essential nutrients.

A BARF diet is essentially a raw diet which is as varied as possible, including lots of raw meaty bones such as chicken wings, chicken necks, rabbit, oxtail, minced meats, lamb shanks, eggs and their shells, liver, heart, fish, yoghurt, vegetables, which have been pulped and fruit. Garlic is also included in the diet, but not all agree with this.

There are those who do not advocate the BARF diet, but there are many who do and I can honestly say that I have come across many dedicated dog breeders who absolutely swear by it, so this may well be something to consider when coming to a decision about what you will feed your Jack Russell.

The clever Jack Russell is a notorious thief – so you need to be on guard to prevent your dog stealing food that may harm him.

FOODS THAT MAY HARM

Chocolate is perhaps most widely known as a food that is toxic to dogs and it is said also to be carcinogenic (cancer causing). It contains theobromine, which is a cardiac stimulant and diuretic; the latter can cause a Jack Russell, or any other dog, to pass large volumes of water and to be unusually thirsty. A dog can become excited and hyperactive, probably with vomiting and diarrhoea. The theobromine will either increase the dog's heart rate, or can cause the heart to beat irregularly, so death can be a consequence, especially during exercise.

Even when a dog has eaten a large quantity of chocolate he may appear well for several hours, but from the onset of sickness, death can occur within twenty-four hours. Cocoa powder and cooking chocolate are the most toxic form, followed by semi-sweet chocolate and dark chocolate. Least dangerous is milk chocolate, an averaged sized dog needing to eat over 250 gms to have any effect. Obviously canine chocolates are of a completely different make-up and can be fed freely, though no treat should be given in excess.

Drinks and foods containing caffeine can cause many of the same symptoms as those derived from eating chocolate, so coffee, coffee grounds, tea and tea bags should also be kept out of harm's way and not offered to your Jack Russell.

There are contradictory reports as to which foods can cause harm to a dog. Garlic, for example is often incorporated into the BARF diet and is used to control intestinal parasites, but others say that garlic is dangerous for Jack Russells and other dogs because it contains thiosulphate, which can cause sickness in both dogs and cats. Onions though, which contain the same ingredient, are a greater danger.

The result of onion toxicity is that a pet goes down with gastroenteritis, vomiting and diarrhoea, caused by haemolytic anaemia, which causes the dog's red blood cells to burst. These burst blood cells can appear in the urine, by which time the dog has become dull, weak and breathless. This problem can be caused when a Jack Russell eats a single large quantity of onions, or repeated meals containing small amounts, so it is certainly wise to give onions a wide berth. Although garlic contains the same toxic ingredient, very large amounts would need to be eaten to cause illness.

Macadamia nuts can also be problematic for dogs and this applies to these nuts whether raw or roasted. Although the toxic compound is unknown, dogs can develop a tremor of the skeletal muscles and weakness or even paralysis in the hindquarters. These symptoms have been observed even in dogs having eaten as few as six kernels.

Walnuts can also cause

problems, as can other nuts, so it is best to avoid nuts with your Jack Russell for they are generally not good for dogs and their high phosphorous content can possibly lead to bladder stones. Peanut butter seems to be the exception to the rule, but only salt and sugar free organic peanut butter should be fed to dogs.

Obviously cooked bones can create serious intestinal problems if they splinter, chicken and lamb bones being potentially the most harmful. All fish and pork products should be well cooked prior to feeding and again, be certain to remove all bones, but it is wiser not to feed tuna as this has a high mercury content. Totally raw and cooked meats should not be fed within the same meal as they digest at different rates.

Most dogs love fruits, but these too can have their dangers. Grapes and raisins should never be fed as they can cause kidney failure; indeed even as little as a single serving of raisins can kill a small dog the size of a Jack Russell. Other fruits, such as apples and peaches are good for dogs, but their seeds actually contain cyanide which of course is poisonous to humans and to dogs too! Whilst as humans we

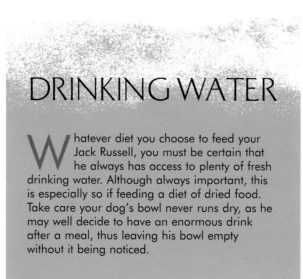

DRINKING WATER

Whatever diet you choose to feed your Jack Russell, you must be certain that he always has access to plenty of fresh drinking water. Although always important, this is especially so if feeding a diet of dried food. Take care your dog's bowl never runs dry, as he may well decide to have an enormous drink after a meal, thus leaving his bowl empty without it being noticed.

throw away the core of an apple, dogs do not know this and can easily ingest the seeds, so be sure to remove the dangerous parts of fruits before feeding them to your terrier.

Tomatoes of course are also fruits, but they can cause tremors and heart arrhythmias; it is actually the stems and leaves that are the most toxic, but the tomatoes themselves are not entirely safe either. In the case of avocados, fruit, stone and plant are all toxic; these can cause fluid accumulation in the chest, abdomen and heart, with difficulty in breathing. Nutmeg should be avoided too, for this can cause tremors, seizures and even death.

Another human food that can be deadly for dogs is the mushroom, so never let your Jack Russell chew on mushrooms that appear in your

garden or in the fields. Certain ones are safe, but not all, so it is better not to take the chance. Honey and molasses may be given in small quantities (but not to dogs with cancer), but sugar and corn syrups should be avoided.

Because dogs have a shorter digestive tract than humans, they are less likely to suffer food poisoning, but still one should take care and avoid feeding stale foods and eggs that are past their 'use by' date. Eggs can be given, but when raw it is better to give only the yolk than the entire egg, though if feeding the BARF diet, even egg shells are fed to dogs!

Fried foods are not ideal for dogs for excessive fat can cause pancreatitis, so animal fats should not be fed in too great a quantity.

DIET FOR THE INFIRM OR ELDERLY

Dogs that are unwell will most probably need some alteration to their diet and your vet can advise on this. Following an operation it is normal to keep a dog on freshly cooked chicken or fish for a couple of days, probably with a little well-cooked brown rice, which is highly nourishing. As the dog recovers from his operation his normal food can gradually be re-introduced.

GUARDING AGAINST OBESITY

Sentimentality is a frequent reason why dogs are allowed to become overweight. There are times when table scraps can be fed to dogs, possibly as a little treat, but they should never be fed to excess. Scraps that are given must be suitable for a dog to eat and of course, small cooked bones should never be given.

There are severe health implications for a dog carrying excess weight. This includes heart and respiratory problems, diabetes and orthopaedic problems such as rupture of the cruciate ligaments. This may either present itself as gradually worsening lameness of the hind leg, or it may be of sudden onset. Often this requires surgical intervention, only going to show how important it is that your Jack Russell does not become overweight.

Jack Russells can be particularly prone to weight gain from around seven years onwards. This can put your dog's health at serious risk and can undoubtedly shorten his life. Your terrier's metabolism will slow down with age, which can cause over-eating to become a problem. You should check his weight frequently throughout his life, so you know if he is gaining a few pounds, or worse still, kilos! You should be able to feel his hips and when you look down at your dog from above, his body should curve inwards slightly beyond the ribcage.

It is also important to mention that obesity should be controlled during puppyhood, for if the number of fat cells in the body is increased during the early stages of life, the dog will be predisposed to obesity during adulthood.

Work out how much food your dog needs – and do not feed any more than his daily ration.

Kidney and heart failure are common in older dogs and it is generally accepted that it is prudent to avoid feeding the adult dog too much protein, sodium (salt) and phosphorous in an endeavour to avoid such problems. Over-feeding of these nutrients can in fact, be detrimental to dogs, even before there is any evidence of disease. Salt retention contributes toward fluid retention, dropsy and swelling of the limbs (odema).

Older dogs tend to be best fed on smaller meals, so they may have two or even three smallish meals spread throughout the day. As they become less active with old age, protein content can usually be reduced. But if you have any doubts at all about what is right for your dog, seek advice from your vet or from a canine nutritionist.

COAT CARE

Whether your Jack Russell has a smooth, broken or rough coat, coat care is an integral part of good maintenance. You should get your young Jack Russell used to regular grooming sessions and soon he will look forward to the experience. A grooming session is a fine time to build up a rapport with your terrier, for this is a time when you will be concentrating 100 per cent on him and he will appreciate this. It also provides a good opportunity to check him over for any minor injuries or parasites you may not otherwise notice.

All Jack Russells need regular brushing, but those with slightly

As a dog grows older, his metabolism slows down and nutritional needs will change.

longer coats will need a little more. Grooming helps to keep the skin healthy, while removing dead hair and promoting new coat growth. Grooming sessions need not be long, though the broken and rough coated terriers require more time and will benefit from hand-stripping.

GENERAL GROOMING PRACTICE

A key to successful grooming is to get your Jack Russell into the habit from a very young age so that he learns to accept the attention. When fully grown, grooming twice weekly should suffice as Jack Russells are pretty

The amount of grooming your Jack Russell needs depends on his coat type.

bathing it is important to wet the coat thoroughly before applying shampoo and of course the water must never be too hot. Always test the water on the back of your own hand before it touches your dog. Also, be careful to rinse off every residue of the shampoo, for if left in the coat it will cause the skin to become dry and can cause dandruff.

GROOMING EQUIPMENT

Many of the items below can be purchased from good pet stores, but some of the rather less usual grooming aids, such as a hound brush, are more easily available from dog shows, or even over the internet from a reputable pet grooming supplier.

- **Slicker brush:** This is a fine wire brush that is extremely helpful for removing dead hair. Some slicker brushes are softer than others and on a young puppy you should use a softer one. Never be too harsh with a slicker-brush for it can easily scratch the skin if you brush too forcefully.
- **Hound glove:** This has a hard side, made of horsehair or something similar and it fits over your hand like a glove. Provided that you always go over the coat in the direction of coat growth, this is a more gentle method of removing dead hair and gives the dog a very enjoyable massage, while helping the coat to look spick and span.
- **Standard metal comb:** This has two sections of teeth, one more widely spaced than the

good at keeping themselves clean. However, during the moulting season, when your Jack Russell is shedding coat, you would be well advised to increase the frequency, not only for dog's sake but also for your own if you don't want too many hairs around your home.

Because of the nature of a Jack Russell's coat, bathing should only be done a couple of times a year and the sort of shampoo needed is not one that will soften the coat. Flea shampoo, or one especially designed for terrier coats, is ideal. Between baths a

waterless shampoo may be used to keep your Jack Russell looking clean. Another useful way of cleaning up and freshening small areas of the coat, such as around the face and back-end when necessary, is to use a mouthwash, diluted one-to-two with water.

Those who show their Jack Russell Terriers, however, like to bath their dogs roughly five days before a show, thus giving the coat sufficient time to settle down and regain its texture in time for the big event. If bathed immediately before a show, the coat will appear too soft. When

GROOMING

If you work through the coat with a hound glove it will loosen dead hair and remove dirt and debris.

A comb through is needed for rough-coated dogs.

other. This you will use to comb your dog through after the coat has been brushed out. You will usually need only the wide-toothed section on the body, but may find the finer teeth handy for the head area and in awkward places such as under the legs.

• **Flea comb:** This is not only useful for checking for any sign of flea infestation, but also helps to keep the short coat flat.

• **Stripping stone:** This is made of black lava and is an excellent tool for removing dead hair, pulling the soft undercoat from beneath. Simply rub the stone on the dead hair and it comes off on the stripping stone.

• **Blunt-nosed scissors:** These will be needed for trimming the hair between the pads of the feet.

• **Thinning scissors and thinning shears:** These are used to tidy up the coat, especially on broken or rough coats. Obviously it is essential that you learn to use scissors correctly from someone more experienced than yourself when you first have your Jack Russell. Scissoring that shows can completely ruin a terrier's appearance.

• **Stripping knife:** This is used to strip out dead hair. There are different blade sizes depending on what is required, so you will need to seek expert

advice. However, those who really want to set off their Jack Russell's coat to best advantage will learn to hand strip with their fingers, rather than use such tools (see page 80).

• **Canine nail clippers/grinder:** Some dogs' nails wear down more quickly than others, usually if they are exercised on hard surfaces, especially concrete. But the majority of dogs will need to have their nails trimmed. When using nail clippers, make sure you do not cut into the quick as this will result in bleeding and it will be very sore for your Jack Russell. A grinder is a safer option when trimming nails, though some dogs do not like the sound as they tend to be quite noisy.

- **Toothbrush/ toothpaste:** You can buy a long handled toothbrush, or you may find it easier to use a finger brush when you are cleaning your Jack Russell's teeth. Toothpaste is specially manufactured for dogs using a variety of meaty flavours.

A stripping stone is an effective tool for removing dead hair.

REGULAR CHECKS

TEETH

Your Jack Russell's teeth should be checked on a weekly basis, nd this includes the gums. If tartar is allowed to build up on the teeth, gum disease will result and this can lead to all manner of health problems, which can even become fatal. Teeth may also become decayed and loose, so tooth loss is the result of cavities and periodontal disease.

Teeth can be professionally scaled by your vet, or experienced owners sometimes do this themselves, though tooth-scaling is not for the novice owner. However, there is a lot you can do to prevent this happening.

There are many kinds of dental chew sticks now available from pet stores and these, given once a day, will undoubtedly help to keep tartar at bay. Safe, raw bones are also very helpful in keeping the teeth clean, but do take care to remove them from your Jack Russell when they have been chewed down to something small enough to swallow and always remove them if shards of bone break off. Personally, I always find raw carrots a useful aid to keeping teeth clean; most dogs love them and there is the additional bonus of a dog getting a tasty treat without putting on excess weight!

Tooth cleaning is something you will need to get your Jack Russell used to from puppyhood, as not all dogs take kindly to it - – though some do as they seem to like the taste of toothpaste.

EARS

You should check ears regularly, especially if your Jack Russell is a working terrier. The very fact that he has foraged about in the undergrowth and down tunnels, makes it more likely that his ears can be affected. Two obvious signs that there is something wrong are shaking of the head or a smell, the latter possibly coupled with a brown discharge. Scratching behind the ear can also be very significant, but this could be for other reasons. It could indeed be fleas, for they have a tendency to nestle in warm spots, such as behind the ear, or in the case of a puppy scratching, it may just be a sign that he is teething. The inside of a Jack Russell's ear should be a pleasant pinky shade, but not bright pink and it should not be too hot to the touch.

Ears can be cleaned regularly using a simple canine ear cleaner, applied inside the ear on a cotton wool pad – but do not delve too deeply into the ear for fear of damaging the ear drum. If infection has set in, a visit to your vet will be necessary and you will have to treat the ear with special ear drops. Some dogs tend to be more susceptible to ear problems than others.

Because they are inquisitive little dogs and fairly low to the

REGULAR CHECKS

Teeth should be checked on a regular basis and cleaned if necessary.

The tips of the nails should be trimmed, taking care not to cut into the quick.

ground, Jack Russells are also rather prone to getting grass seeds stuck down the ear. These get caught in the hair and if not spotted soon enough can easily burrow down causing problems until they are extracted. If left untreated they may even pierce the ear drum – just one of the reasons why a regular ear check is very necessary.

EYES
Your Jack Russell's eyes must be kept clean and should be checked on a daily basis. It an

easy matter to wipe the inner corners with a damp cotton pad, thus preventing a build up of matter. If the eyes have a tendency to constantly run, this could be due to a tear duct blockage, or maybe an allergy, so veterinary advice must be sought.

NAILS AND FEET
Keep a regular check on nails and feet and take prompt action if your Jack Russell shows signs of limping. It is important to train your dog to accept his feet being inspected from a very young age,

for if not attended to until maturity, you will probably have a very wriggly Jack Russell on your hands!

Because of their white coat, most Jack Russells have white nails, which makes it easy to see the quick when trimming, but on dark nails you should take off only a very little at a time, allowing the quick to recede. It is really a matter of personal preference whether you use guillotine clippers or straight edged ones, but it is essential that you are able to see exactly where you are clipping and never use a blunt set.

If by mistake you cut into the quick and cause the nail to bleed, you must immediately apply a blood stop powder, or if by chance you don't have any to hand, you can rub a bar of softened soap over the end of the nail.

Some pet owners can find nail trimming a little difficult; if this is the case, your vet will be happy to trim them for you for a small fee, but this must be done regularly.

You will also need to check the pads of the feet to be sure nothing has become wedged between them and that there are no cuts on the bottom of the feet. This is another place where grass seeds can do their worst. If your Jack Russell is broken or rough coated, you will also need to trim excess coat from between the pads which can cause discomfort. You can also trim the hair around the feet so they look neat and tidy. This is particularly important if you plan to show your terrier, as the judge will expect the feet to be nice and tight; careful trimming can enhance this.

STRIPPING A JACK RUSSELL'S COAT

The best way to control the coat of either a broken coated or rough coated Jack Russell is by hand stripping, though if you keep your dog only as a pet you may prefer to use a professional dog groomer, who will almost certainly use electric clippers.

Hand stripping takes a great deal of time and is not a viable proposition for a groomer, unless of course they are presenting for the show ring. However, if you want your terrier to be presented to absolute perfection and yet still retain that 'natural look', hand stripping will be essential. Although a clipped coat can still look good and very neat, the clippers just take the ends off the hairs that would otherwise be shed, leaving a sharp end to each hair. Over time, hand-stripping will certainly improve the hard coat texture, even on a coat of less good quality.

Another method of controlling the coat is by using a stripping knife to take out the loose coat, but again this can only be used in moderation, or for difficult areas if a dog is destined for the show ring. A stripping knife if used to excess or as an alternative to hand-stripping, will never give such a natural appearance to the coat and after all, the Jack Russell is meant to be a very natural breed.

When hand stripping, the coat should easily come away when pulled. If it does not, this means that the coat is not ready to come out and should be left a while, perhaps for another couple of weeks.

Hopefully you will have trained your Jack Russell to stand on a table for weekly grooming and routine checks. The table must be steady and should have a non-slip surface, so your dog feels secure and confident. You can purchase various kinds of

specially made grooming tables from dog shows or you may prefer to place a piece of rubber matting on top of a table you already have at home. Working with your dog on a table is essential when hand stripping.

If you are not showing your Jack Russell, it is possible that you will only need to strip out the coat thoroughly once each year. This annual session will probably take about three hours, slightly less for a thoroughly professional groomer. Nonetheless, this is a long time for a dog to be standing on a table, so some people prefer to break the stripping procedure down into several shorter sessions, until the desired result is achieved. It is important that your dog does not get over-tired or agitated by this procedure, for grooming should always be a pleasurable experience, both for dog and owner.

STEP BY STEP GUIDE
- Start by thoroughly brushing the coat using a slicker brush, making sure you groom against the lie of the coat, that is to say in the opposite direction from the tail.
- Repeat the process using a comb. This will result in the majority of the loose undercoat and topcoat being removed.
- The remaining dead hair will have to be removed by hand, using your finger and thumb to pull out the long hairs of the topcoat. Your hands must always be clean.
- Begin at the neck, brushing the

STRIPPING THE COAT

This is a time consuming procedure, but it keeps your dog's coat in order while retaining a natural look.

Hand stripping is a process where finger and thumb are used to gently pull dead hair from the coat.

Work from the neck down to the chest.

Continue along the top and sides of the body.

81

The hindquarters require attention.

Finish off by stripping the tail.

coat upward; grip the longer hairs and pull them out in a positive fashion, but always pull in the direction in which the coat is growing.

• To make the procedure easier by allowing a better grip, you can dust a little hard chalk over the coat. As you proceed, you will begin to see that your broken or rough coated Jack Russell begins to resemble a short-haired one, for it is primarily the undercoat that has been left in place and it is on neck and shoulders that the topcoat will most probably have been longest.

• Use the same method along the dog's body and sides.

• The hair on the legs will be shorter, so will require less attention.

• Around the feet the longest hairs should be stripped out by hand and then trimmed on the outside edges of the toes with blunt-ended scissors to complete the picture.

• A rough coated Jack Russell will have substantially more hair under the belly and tail than does the broken coat, so these areas may need attention. They are usually more sensitive than most other areas, so do please take care not to hurt your Jack Russell and never lose your patience. Keep stripping away, bit by bit, in the direction of coat growth, not forgetting the insides of the thighs.

• Scissors can be used to finish off, with blunt-ended scissors used very carefully around the genitals. Just keep in mind though, that on a Jack Russell, scissors should only be used around toes and genitalia; in this way a thoroughly natural appearance will be maintained.

After a full hand strip, it will take roughly nine weeks for the coat to grow in again properly and during this period you should continue to brush and comb your terrier normally, ideally rubbing the coat over, just with damp hands, before you start. This will loosen the dead hair. Any coat that is shed at this time will be the undercoat which, in consequence, will make way for the new coat to grow through. Within another three weeks or so, your Jack Russell will have a healthy, thick new coat, of which both he and you will be thoroughly proud!

TRIMMING THE COAT

Thinning scissors are used to give a smooth contour to the neck.

Trim along the underside.

Thinning scissors are used on the hindquarters.

SHOW PRESENTATION

If you intend to show your Jack Russell in conformation classes, it is highly important that your exhibit does not look over-trimmed. This is essentially a natural breed, so the coat should not be trimmed in such a way as to make your dog to look over-exaggerated. Having said that, if you understand the conformation of your dog, you can, with expertise, use careful coat presentation to bring out the best features of your dog and to lessen the appearance of any faults there may be in construction. Which of the three coat types your terrier has should be clearly evident and your dog should never appear sculpted in outline, so in an ideal world, trimming should not be necessary. A very profuse coat on a Jack Russell is not desirable at all and profuse feathering is uncharacteristic; after all this is a working terrier and was not created as a 'show piece'.

For the show ring very little coat should need to be removed prior to a show, except perhaps a few tufts of hair that may have grown up on top of the head and maybe a few hairs that have grown upward near the inner corners of the eye. On broken and rough coated Jack Russells, the eyebrows and moustache are characteristic of the breed and should under no circumstances be removed.

Tail length on the Jack Russell should complement the body, so it is an owner's prerogative either to leave the hair on the end or to trim it shorter, whichever you feel enhances the balance of your dog. Stray hair on the underside of the tail should be discreetly trimmed and it is wise to remove any excess hair around the anal area.

When entering shows, you will have to calculate the time at which your dog will have his annual major hand strip, for it would be unwise to exhibit your dog until the new coat has had a little time to grow in. In the case of a puppy, the full coat will not develop until around the age of a year, so should not need any major attention before then. However, you should always carry out a regular routine of brief grooming sessions, in part to get him used to the procedure, but also to maintain his coat in tip-top condition.

Exercise that involves physical exertion and mental stimulation is ideal for the Jack Russell.

EXERCISE

A Jack Russell Terrier that is used for work will inevitably get plenty of exercise of the correct kind, but it is always important never to let him bed down wet or dirty, as not only will this be very uncomfortable for the night, but will almost certainly give rise to aches and pains in later life.

Equally a Jack Russell that takes part regularly in Agility, Flyball or Heelwork to Music will also get plenty of exercise of the right kind, for he will be provided with physical and mental stimulation. But if a Jack Russell is simply kept as a pet, which many are, it is important that regular exercise is given. A Jack Russell has a particularly lively mind, so both brain and body will need to be exercised well if he is to remain a happy and contented family pet. If you do not want a restless Jack Russell roaming around your sitting room at night, you must make sure he has had enough to do during the day.

Of course he will make his own exercise and amusement in your garden, but he will also need a couple of brisk lead walks each day, which will also provide you, his owner, with an enjoyable breath of fresh air. As terriers are designed to hunt, do not let him off the lead unless you know that he is in a very safe place, or if you have every confidence that he will return to you immediately you call him back. Many a terrier has been lost down a hole, sometimes for days and not always with a happy ending.

Many Jack Russells also enjoy swimming, which provides wonderful exercise, provided the dog is allowed only to swim in a safe place and under close supervision. Swimming is a great way to use up energy in a controlled manner and can be a good way to cool off during the summer months. Again, make sure that your Jack Russell is dried off thoroughly before bedtime.

THE IN SEASON BITCH

Jack Russells generally follow the usual pattern of the majority of breeds, coming into season roughly twice a year. It may not be exactly at six month intervals, but probably between six and eight. The season lasts for approximately 21 days, though can occasionally be a few days longer.

Although there is a vaginal swelling and red discharge, which lightens in colour as the season progresses, Jack Russells usually like to keep themselves very clean, so it is possible for owners not to notice the season during its first few days. This can sometimes cause a bit of a dilemma if you are planning to mate your bitch.

Obviously during her season, a bitch must be kept totally away from males, not only to prevent an unwanted pregnancy, but also to avoid the dog being too worried about a bitch being around in full heat. Just occasionally a bitch can have very little swelling and almost no discharge, often known as a 'silent season'. This makes it very difficult to know when she is actually on heat. Owners need to keep a very careful eye on such bitches to prevent accidental matings – keeping an accurate diary is always a good idea. In fact, diary keeping is always useful, for it is all too easy to forget exactly which month your bitch came in season last. This will also help you to plan ahead for holidays and such like.

FALSE PREGNANCIES
Even though a bitch may not have been mated, there is still a chance that she may have what is known as a 'false pregnancy' and some bitches are more prone to this than others. Approaching the time that she would normally be due to whelp, she can go through all the motions, producing milk, preparing her nest and even sometimes putting on weight. If you are at all concerned about her condition, possibly thinking she may have been mated accidentally when you weren't about, do take her along to your vet for a check up.

I have very occasionally had a bitch who has had 'false pregnancies' and have found that the homoeopathic remedy Pulsatilla has sorted her out quite easily.

CARING FOR THE OLDER DOG
The Jack Russell is a long-lived breed and hopefully, will remain in the best of health for many years. However, eventually time

Close supervision is essential when a bitch is in season.

takes is toll on any dog's system and as a loving owner you should be there to ensure that the last few years of his life are as comfortable and enjoyable as they can possibly be.

Many Jack Russells who live a particularly long time, lose weight with age, but dietary control can help this. The older dog will appreciate more frequent, smaller meals, probably two or three

The older dog deserves special care and consideration.

Always keep a careful check on your older dog's overall condition too. Be on the alert for any odorous breath, which probably indicates dental disease, or it may just be that as the gaps between the teeth have widened with age, they may have trapped small pieces of food which will need to be removed. Look out also for any signs of abscesses in the mouth; these often occur at the very back of the mouth and may be noticed by a swelling under the eye. A sign that your elderly Jack Russell is experiencing discomfort in the mouth is if he scrapes his head sideways along the ground, or along the bottom of your furniture.

Because he is taking less exercise, his nails will probably grow longer than they normally do, for they will not be worn down so much. So keep a check on these and clip more frequently than usual. Alternatively you may of course take your terrier along to the vet who will see to this for a small fee.

Another problem with the older dog is that his bladder probably won't work so efficiently as it did in the days of his youth. Sometimes this is a just a leakage of urine during the night, which can be helped by not allowing him to drink water after about 7 or 8pm, depending on your bed-time routine. Drugs are also available to help this situation. If there is frequent passing of urine both during the day and night, a urine sample and possibly a blood test will need to be taken by your vet, as this may indicate

times a day. This will help absorption and digestion. On the other hand, the Jack Russell that is overweight, possibly due to taking less exercise in his later years, will need his dietary intake controlled for he will need fewer calories. This is because he now lives a more sedentary life than in earlier years; he will be burning up fewer calories in his daily activities, which probably revolve more around walking around the home and lazing by the fireside.

Several special diets are available for the older dog; these are usually higher in fibre and lower in energy than needed by younger animals. Some can be obtained from the manufacturer, but others are prescription only diets, available from your vet. In any case, if you at all unsure about your dog's health in older age, veterinary advice should always be sought.

a different problem.

The older dog must always have comfortable housing conditions and bedding must always be thoroughly dry. This of course is always necessary, but more so in old age when arthritis can become a bit of a problem for your dog. Very importantly, he must never feel that his nose is being pushed out of joint. He has given you many faithful years of companionship and the fact that he is not now so sprightly as he used to be should in no way diminish the love you have shared between you.

LETTING GO

Sadly the time will eventually come when you will have to part with your dog, due to infirmity which is no longer making his life worthwhile, or because of an incurable disease. This is a most distressing time for you and your family, but unfortunately, a dog's life being so much shorter than our own, it is inevitable.

I suppose we all wish that our dogs would just die peacefully in their sleep one day, but unfortunately this rarely happens, leaving us with the dreadful decision about when is the right time to let your Jack Russell be put to sleep. This is something you will have to discuss with your vet and if you have built up a rapport with him over your dog's life, hopefully you will feel able to trust his advice.

You can of course take your dog along to the vet to say your last goodbyes, but equally you could ask your vet to come to your home, depending on your dog's condition. Try to keep your tears until after he has closed his eyes for the last time and talk to him all the time to give him comfort and let him know you are there. I always like to be with my dogs when they are put to sleep, and in most cases they just peacefully drift off to another world. But if you feel you cannot control your emotions, it is probably better to say goodbye before passing your dog over to your vet, who will deal with this in a caring but professional manner.

It is never easy to offer advice as to what to dog with your dog after he has died, but personally I have all mine cremated individually. Yes, this costs a little money, but in my estimation all my dogs have been worth every penny, and I can do with their ashes what I will. Communal cremations cost rather less and of course you may simply leave your dog in the hands of the vet for disposal according to his practice. A dog that has died or been put to sleep at a vet's cannot legally be returned to you for burial, so if this is your desire your vet will have to visit your home unless, if you have been lucky, your dog has died in his sleep.

Whatever the end, you will surely have many happy memories to cherish forever.

In time you will be able to look back and remember all the happy times you spent with your beloved Jack Russell.

TRAINING AND SOCIALISATION

Chapter 6

When you decided to bring a Jack Russell into your life, you probably had dreams of how it was going to be: long walks together, cosy evenings with a Jack Russell lying devotedly at your feet and whenever you returned home, there would always be a special welcome waiting for you.

There is no doubt that you can achieve all this – and much more – with a Jack Russell, but like anything that is worth having, you must be prepared to put in the work. A Jack Russell regardless of whether he is a puppy or an adult, does not come ready trained, understanding exactly what you want and fitting perfectly into your lifestyle. A Jack Russell has to learn his place in your family and he must discover what is acceptable behaviour.

We have a great starting point in that the breed has an out-going temperament. The Jack Russell was developed to be a working terrier and although he retains a tough, fearless outlook on life, he also enjoys interacting with his human family . He is also highly intelligent; he is quick to learn so you must be on your mettle in order to bring out the best in him.

THE FAMILY PACK

Dogs have been domesticated for some 14,000 years, but luckily for us, they have inherited and retained behaviour from their distant ancestor – the wolf. A Jack Russell may never have lived in the wild, but he is born with the survival skills and the mentality of a meat-eating predator who hunts in a pack. A wolf living in a pack owes its existence to mutual co-operation and an acceptance of a hierarchy, as this ensures both food and protection. A domesticated dog living in a family pack has exactly the same outlook. He wants food, companionship, and leadership – and it is your job to provide for these needs.

YOUR ROLE

Theories about dog behaviour and methods of training go in and out of fashion, but in reality, nothing has changed from the day when wolves ventured in from the wild to join the family circle. The wolf (and equally the dog) accepts a subservient place in the family pack in return for food and protection. In a dog's eyes, you are his leader and he relies on you to make all the important decisions. This does not mean that you have to act like a dictator or a bully. You are accepted as a leader, without argument, as long as you have the right credentials.

The first part of the job is easy. You are the provider and you are therefore respected because you supply food. In a Jack Russell's eyes, you must be the ultimate hunter, because a day never goes by when you cannot find food. The second part of the leader's job description is straightforward, but for some reason we find it hard to achieve. In order for a dog to accept his place in the family pack, he must respect his leader as the decision-maker. A low-ranking pack animal does not question authority; he is perfectly happy to see someone else shoulder the responsibility. Problems will only arise if you cut a poor figure as leader and the dog feels he should mount a challenge for the top-ranking role.

HOW TO BE A GOOD LEADER

There are a number of guidelines to follow to establish yourself in the role of leader in a way that your Jack Russell understands and respects. If you have a puppy, you may think you don't have to take this on board for a few months, but that would be a big mistake. With a Jack Russell it is absolutely essential to start as you mean to go on. The behaviour he learns as a puppy will continue throughout his

Have you got what it takes to be a firm, fair and consistent leader?

adult life, which means that undesirable behaviour can be very difficult to rectify.

When your Jack Russell first arrives in his new home, follow these guidelines:

- **Keep it simple:** Decide on the rules you want your Jack Russell to obey and always make it 100 per cent clear what is acceptable and what is unacceptable, behaviour.

- **Be consistent:** If you are not consistent about enforcing rules, how can you expect your Jack Russell to take you seriously? There is nothing worse than allowing your Jack Russell to jump on the sofa one moment and then scolding him the next time he does it because he is muddy. As far as the Jack Russell is concerned, he may as well try it on

because he can't predict your reaction. Bear in mind, inconsistency leads to insecurity.

- **Get your timing right:** If you are rewarding your Jack Russell and equally if you are reprimanding him, you must respond within one to two seconds otherwise the dog will not link his behaviour with your reaction (see page 93).

- **Read your dog's body language:** Find out how to read body language and facial expressions (see page 91) so that you understand your Jack Russell's feelings and intentions.

- **Be aware of your own body language:** When you ask your Jack Russell to do something, do not bend over him and talk to him at eye level. Assert your authority by standing over him and keeping an upright posture. You can also help your dog to learn by using your body language to communicate with him. For example, if you want your dog to come to you, open your arms out and look inviting. If you want your dog to stay, use a hand signal (palm flat, facing the dog) so you are effectively 'blocking' his advance.

- **Tone of voice:** Dogs do not speak English; they learn by associating a word with the required action. However, they are very receptive to tone of voice, so you can use your voice to praise him or to correct undesirable behaviour. If you are pleased with your Jack Russell, praise him to the skies in a warm, happy voice. If you want to stop him raiding the bin, use a deep, stern voice when you say "No".

- **Give one command only:** If you keep repeating a command, or keeping changing it, your Jack Russell will think you are babbling and will probably ignore you. If your Jack Russell does not respond the first time you ask, make it simple by using a treat to lure him into position and then you can reward him for a correct response.
- **Daily reminders:** A young, cheeky Jack Russell is apt to forget his manners from time to time and an adolescent dog may attempt to challenge your authority (see page 105). Rather than coming down on your Jack Russell like a ton of bricks when he does something wrong, try to prevent bad manners by daily reminders of good manners. For example:
  i.   Do not let your dog barge ahead of you when you are going through a door.
  ii. Do not let him leap out of the car the moment you open the door (which could be potentially lethal, as well as being disrespectful).
  iii. Do not let him eat from your hand when you are at the table.

Keep it simple so that your dog understands what you want.

iv. Do not let him 'win' a toy at the end of a play session and then make off with it. You 'own' his toys and you 'allow' him to play with them. Your Jack Russell must learn to give up a toy when you ask.

UNDERSTANDING YOUR JACK RUSSELL

Body language is an important means of communication between dogs, which they use to make friends, to assert status and to avoid conflict. It is important to get on your dog's wavelength by understanding his body language and reading his facial expressions.

- A positive body posture and a wagging tail indicate a happy, confident dog.

- A crouched body posture with ears back and tail down show that a dog is being submissive. A dog may do this when he is being told off or if a more assertive dog approaches him.
- A bold dog will stand tall, looking strong and alert. His ears will be forward and his tail will be held high.
- A dog who raises his hackles (lifting the fur along his topline) is trying to look as scary as possible.
- A playful dog will go down on his front legs while standing on his hind legs in a bow position. This friendly invitation says: "I'm no threat, let's play."
- A dominant, aggressive dog will meet other dogs with a hard stare. If he is challenged, he may bare his teeth and growl

You can learn a lot from watching dogs meeting and greeting. This Jack Russell has understood that the big dog's intentions are entirely friendly, and he is not intimidated – despite the difference in size.

and the corners of his mouth will be drawn forward. His ears will be forward and he will appear tense in every muscle.

- A nervous dog will often show aggressive behaviour as a means of self-protection. If threatened, this dog will lower his head and flatten his ears. The corners of his mouth may be drawn back and he may bark or whine.

- Some Jack Russells are 'smilers', curling up their top lip and showing their teeth when they greet people. This should never be confused with a snarl, which would be accompanied by the upright posture of a dominant dog. A smiling dog will have a low body posture and a wagging tail; he is being submissive and it is a greeting that is often

used when low-ranking animals greet high-ranking animals in a pack.

GIVING REWARDS

Why should your Jack Russell do as you ask? If you follow the guidelines given above, your Jack Russell should respect your authority, but what about the time when he is playing with a new doggy friend or has found a really enticing scent? The answer is that you must always be the most interesting, the most attractive and the most irresistible person in your Jack Russell's eyes. It would be nice to think that you could achieve this by personality alone, but most of us need a little extra help. You need to find out what is the biggest reward for your dog. In most cases, a Jack Russell will be

motivated to work for food reward, although some prefer a game with a toy. Jack Russells that are trained to compete in Agility or Flyball are often stimulated by chasing after a ball and this will be seen as a high value reward. But whatever reward you use, make sure it is something that your dog really wants.

When you are teaching a dog a new exercise, you should reward your Jack Russell frequently. When he knows the exercise or command, reward him randomly so that he keeps on responding to you in a positive manner.

If your Jack Russell does something extra special, like leaving his canine chum mid-play in the park, make sure he really knows how pleased you are by giving him a handful of treats or

You need to find a reward that your Jack Russell really values.

throwing his ball a few extra times. If he gets a bonanza reward, he is more likely to come back on future occasions because you have proved to be even more rewarding than his previous activity.

TOP TREATS

Some trainers grade treats depending on what they are asking the dog to do. A dog may get a low-grade treat (such as a piece of dry food) to reward good behaviour on a random basis, such as sitting when you open a door or allowing you to examine his teeth. High-grade treats (which may be cooked liver, sausage or cheese) may be reserved for training new exercises, or for use in the park when you want a really good recall, for example.

Whatever type of treat you use, you should remember to subtract it from your Jack Russell's daily food ration. Jack Russells are prone to obesity. Fat dogs are lethargic, prone to health problems and will almost certainly have a shorter life expectancy, so reward your Jack Russell, but always keep a check on his figure!

HOW DO DOGS LEARN?

It is not difficult to get inside your Jack Russell's head and understand how he learns, as it is not dissimilar to the way we learn. Dogs learn by conditioning: they find out that specific behaviours produce specific consequences. This is known as operant conditioning or consequence learning. Consequences have to be

immediate or clearly linked to the behaviour, as a dog sees the world in terms of action and result. Dogs will quickly learn if an action has a bad consequence or a good consequence.

Dogs also learn by association. This is known as classical conditioning or association learning. It is the type of learning made famous by Pavlov's experiment with dogs. Pavlov presented dogs with food and measured their salivary response (how much they drooled). Then he rang a bell just before presenting the food. At first, the dogs did not salivate until the food was presented. But after a while they learnt that the sound of the bell meant that food was coming and so they salivated when they heard the bell. A dog needs to learn the association in

THE CLICKER REVOLUTION

Karen Pryor pioneered the technique of clicker training when she was working with dolphins. It is very much a continuation of Pavlov's work and makes full use of association learning. Karen wanted to mark 'correct' behaviour at the precise moment it happened. She found it was impossible to toss a fish to a dolphin when it was in mid-air, when she wanted to reward it. Her aim was to establish a conditioned response so the dolphin knew that it had performed correctly and a reward would follow.

The solution was the clicker: a small matchbox-shaped training aid, with a metal tongue that makes a click when it is pressed. To begin with, the dolphin had to learn that a click meant that food was coming. The dolphin then learnt that it must 'earn' a click in order to get a reward. Clicker training has been used with many different animals, most particularly with dogs, and it has proved hugely successful. It is a great aid for pet owners and is also widely used by professional trainers who are training highly specialised skills.

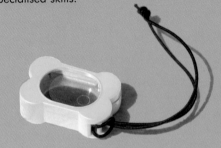

order for it to have any meaning. For example, a dog that has never seen a lead before will be completely indifferent to it. A dog that has learnt that a lead means he is going for a walk will get excited the second he sees the lead; he has learnt to associate a lead with a walk.

BE POSITIVE

The most effective method of training dogs is to use their ability to learn by consequence and to teach that the behaviour you want produces a good consequence. For example, if you ask your Jack Russell to "Sit" and reward him with a treat, he will learn that it is worth his while to sit on command because it will lead to a treat. He is far more likely to repeat the behaviour and the behaviour will become stronger, because it results in a positive outcome. This method of training is known as positive reinforcement and it generally leads to a happy, co-operative dog that is willing to work and a handler who has fun training their dog.

The opposite approach is negative reinforcement. This is far less effective and often results in a poor relationship between dog and owner. In this method of training, you ask your Jack Russell to "Sit" and if he does not respond, you deliver a sharp yank on the training collar or push his rear to the ground. The dog learns that not responding to your command has a bad consequence and he may be less likely to ignore you in the future. However, it may well have a bad consequence for you, too. A dog that is treated in this way may associate harsh handling with the handler and become aggressive or fearful. Instead of establishing a pattern of willing co-operation, you are establishing a relationship built on coercion.

GETTING STARTED

As you train your Jack Russell you will develop your own techniques as you get to know what motivates him. You may decide to get involved with clicker training or you may prefer to go for a simple command-and-reward formula. It does not matter what form of training you use, as long as it is based on positive, reward-based methods.

There are a few important guidelines to bear in mind when you are training your Jack Russell:

- Find a training area that is free from distractions, particularly when you are just starting out. The Jack Russell loves to use his nose, so it may be easier to train him indoors to begin with.
- Keep training sessions short, especially with young puppies that have very short attention spans.
- Do not train if you are in a bad mood or if you are on a tight schedule – the training session will be doomed to failure.
- If you are using a toy as a reward, make sure it is only available when you are training. In this way it has an added value for your Jack Russell.
- If you are using food treats, make sure they are bite-size and easy to swallow; you don't want to hang about while your Jack Russell chews on his treat.
- Do not attempt to train your Jack Russell after he has eaten, or soon after returning from exercise. He will either be too full up to care about food

A Jack Russell is easily distracted, so keep training sessions short and positive.

treats or too tired to concentrate.

- When you are training, move around your allocated area so that your dog does not think that an exercise can only be performed in one place.
- If your Jack Russell is finding an exercise difficult, try not to get frustrated. Go back a step and praise him for his effort. You will probably find he is more successful when you try again at the next training session.
- If a training session is not going well – either because you are in the wrong frame of mind or the dog is not focusing –

ask your Jack Russell to do something you know he can do (such as a trick he enjoys performing) and then you can reward him with a food treat or a play with his favourite toy, ending the session on a happy, positive note.

- Do not train for too long. You need to end a training session on a high, with your Jack Russell wanting more, rather than making him sour by asking too much from him.

In the exercises that follow, clicker training is introduced and followed, but all the exercises will work without the use of a clicker.

Use a treat or a toy so you can lure your dog into a Sit.

INTRODUCING A CLICKER

This is dead easy, and the intelligent Jack Russell will learn about the clicker in record time! It can be combined with attention training, which is a very useful tool and can be used on many different occasions.

- Prepare some treats and go to an area that is free from distractions. Allow your Jack Russell to wander and when he stops to look at you, click and reward by throwing him a treat. This means he will not crowd you, but will go looking for the treat. Repeat a couple of times. If your Jack Russell is very easily distracted, you may need to start this exercise with the dog on a lead.

- After a few clicks, your Jack Russell will understand that if he hears a click, he will get a treat. He must now learn that he must 'earn' a click. This time, when your Jack Russell looks at you, wait a little longer before clicking and then reward him. If your Jack Russell is on a lead but responding well, try him off the lead.

- When your Jack Russell is working for a click and giving you his attention, you can introduce a cue or command word, such as "Watch". Repeat a few times, using the cue. You now have a Jack Russell that understands the clicker and will give you his attention when you ask him to "Watch".

TRAINING EXERCISES

THE SIT

This is the easiest exercise to teach, so it is rewarding for both you and your Jack Russell.

- Choose a tasty treat and hold it just above your puppy's nose. As he looks up at the treat, he will naturally go into the 'Sit'. As soon as he is in position, reward him.

- Repeat the exercise and when your pup understands what you want, introduce the "Sit" command.

- You can practise the Sit exercise at mealtimes by holding out the bowl and waiting for your dog to sit. Most Jack Russells learn this one very quickly!

With practice, your Jack Russell will respond to a verbal cue and will not need to be lured into position.

THE DOWN

Work hard at this exercise because a reliable 'Down' is useful in many different situations, and an instant 'Down' can be a lifesaver.

- You can start with your dog in a 'Sit', or it is just as effective to teach it when the dog is standing. Hold a treat just below your puppy's nose and slowly lower it towards the ground. The treat acts as a lure and your puppy will follow it, first going down on his forequarters and then bringing his hindquarters down as he tries to get the treat.
- Make sure you close your fist around the treat and only reward your puppy with the treat when he is in the correct position. If your puppy is reluctant to go 'Down', you can apply gentle pressure on his shoulders to encourage him to go into the correct position.
- When your puppy is following the treat and going into position, introduce a verbal command.
- Build up this exercise over a period of time, each time waiting a little longer before giving the reward, so the puppy learns to stay in the 'Down' position.

THE RECALL

It is never too soon to begin training your Jack Russell the recall. Remember, this breed is descended from a working terrier whose hunting skills depended on his scenting ability. The instinct to go to ground is also very strong in many Jack Russells and tragically, a dog who fails to respond the recall may go to ground and become trapped, sometimes with fatal consequences.

Hopefully, the breeder will have already started recall training by calling the puppies in from outside and rewarding them with some treats scattered on the floor. But even if this has not been the case, you will find that a puppy arriving in his new home is highly responsive. His chief desire is to follow you and be with you. Capitalise on this from day one by getting your pup's attention and calling him to you in a bright, excited tone of voice.

COMING WHEN CALLED

For a more formal recall, you can start with your dog in a Sit.

Call the dog to you, making yourself sound positive and exciting.

Give your dog a big reward when he comes to you.

SECRET WEAPON

You can build up a strong recall by using another form of association learning. Buy a whistle and when you are giving your Jack Russell his food, peep on the whistle. You can choose the type of signal you want to give: two short peeps or one long whistle, for example. Within a matter of days, your dog will learn that the sound of the whistle means that food is coming.

Now transfer the lesson outside. Arm yourself with some tasty treats and the whistle. Allow your Jack Russell to run free in the garden and after a couple of minutes, use the whistle. The dog has already learnt to associate the whistle with food, so he will come towards you.

Immediately reward him with a treat and lots of praise. Repeat the lesson a few times in the garden, so you are confident that your dog is responding before trying it in the park. Make sure you always have some treats in your pocket when you go for a walk and your dog will quickly learn how rewarding it is to come to you.

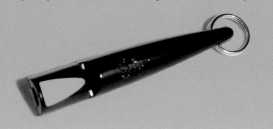

- Practise in the garden. When your puppy is busy exploring, get his attention by calling his name and as he runs towards you, introduce the verbal command "Come". Make sure you sound happy and exciting, so your puppy wants to come to you. When he responds, give him lots of praise.

- If your puppy is slow to respond, try running away a few paces, or jumping up and down. It doesn't matter how silly you look, the key issue is to get your puppy's attention and then make yourself irresistible!

- In a dog's mind, coming when called should be regarded as the best fun because he knows he is always going to be rewarded. Never make the mistake of telling your dog off, no matter how slow he is to respond, as you will undo all your previous hard work.

- When you call your Jack Russell to you, make sure he comes up close enough to be touched. He must understand that "Come" means that he should come right up to you, otherwise he will think that he can approach and then veer off when it suits him.

- When you are free running your dog, make sure you have his favourite toy or a pocket full of treats so you can reward him at intervals throughout the walk when you call him to you. Do not allow your dog to free run and

only call him back at the end of the walk to clip on his lead. An intelligent Jack Russell will soon realise that the recall means the end of his walk and then end of fun – so who can blame him for not wanting to come back?

TRAINING LINE
This is the equivalent of a very long lead, which you can buy at a pet store, or you can make your own with a length of rope. The training line is attached to your Jack Russell's collar and should be around 15 feet (4.5 metres) in length.

The purpose of the training line is to prevent your Jack Russell from disobeying you so that he never has the chance to get into

The aim is for your Jack Russell to walk on a loose lead, giving attention when requested.

bad habits. For example, when you call your Jack Russell and he ignores you, you can immediately pick up the end of the training line and call him again. By picking up the line you will have attracted his attention and if you call in an excited, happy voice, your Jack Russell will come to you. The moment he reaches you, give him a tasty treat so he is instantly rewarded for making the 'right' decision.

The training line is very useful when your Jack Russell becomes an adolescent and is testing your leadership. When you have reinforced the correct behaviour a number of times, your dog will build up a strong recall and you will not need to use a training line.

WALKING ON A LOOSE LEAD
This is a simple exercise, which baffles many Jack Russell owners. Although the Jack Russell is a small dog, he can be very determined and he can quickly get into the habit of pulling on the lead. In most cases, owners make the mistake of wanting to get on with the expedition rather that training the dog how to walk on a lead.

In this exercise, as with all lessons that you teach your Jack Russell, you must adopt a calm, determined, no-nonsense attitude so he knows that you mean business. This is a dog who will run rings round you unless you earn his respect. Once this is established, your Jack Russell will take you

seriously and be happy to co-operate with you.

- In the early stages of lead training, allow your puppy to pick his route and follow him. He will get used to the feeling of being 'attached' to you and has no reason to put up any resistance.
- Next, find a toy or a tasty treat and show it to your puppy. Let him follow the treat/toy for a few paces and then reward him.
- Build up the amount of time your pup will walk with you and when he is walking nicely by your side, introduce the verbal command "Heel" or "Close". Give lots of praise when your pup is in the correct position.
- When your pup is walking alongside you, keep focusing his attention on you by using his name and then rewarding him when he looks at you. If it is going well, introduce some changes of direction.
- Do not attempt to take your puppy out on the lead until you have mastered the basics at home. You need to be confident that your puppy accepts the lead and will focus his attention on you, when requested, before you face the challenge of a busy environment.
- If you are heading somewhere special, such as the park, your Jack Russell will probably try to pull because he is impatient to get there. If this happens, stop, call your dog to you and do not set off again until he is

in the correct position. It may take time, but your Jack Russell will eventually realise that it is more productive to walk by your side than to pull ahead.

STAYS

This may not be the most exciting exercise, but it is one of the most useful. There are many occasions when you want your Jack Russell to stay in position, even if it is only for a few seconds. The classic example is when you want your Jack Russell to stay in the back of the car until you have clipped on his lead. Some trainers use the verbal command "Stay" when the dog is to stay in position for an extended period of time and "Wait" if the dog is to stay in position for a few seconds until you give the next command. Others trainers use a universal "Stay" to cover all situations. It all comes down to personal preference, and as long as you are consistent, your dog will understand the command he is given.

- Put your puppy in a 'Sit' or a 'Down' and use a hand signal (flat palm, facing the dog) to show he is to stay in position. Step a pace away from the dog. Wait a second, step back and reward him. If you have a lively pup, you may find it easier to train this exercise on the lead.

- Repeat the exercise, gradually increasing the distance you can leave your dog. When you return to your dog's side,

The Jack Russell is not known for his patience, so learning the Stay exercise may take some hard work.

praise him quietly and release him with a command, such as "OK".

- Remember to keep your body language very still when you are training this exercise and avoid eye contact with your dog. Work on this exercise over a period of time and you will build up a really reliable 'Stay'.

SOCIALISATION

While your Jack Russell is mastering basic obedience exercises, there is other, equally important work to do with him. A Jack Russell is not only becoming a part of your home and family, he is becoming a member of the community. He needs to be able to live in the

outside world, coping calmly with every new situation that comes his way. It is your job to introduce him to as many different experiences as possible and to encourage him to behave in an appropriate manner. This is important with all breeds, but it is especially important with a Jack Russell who does not always interact well with other dogs. The more work you put in socialising your Jack Russell with other dogs of sound temperament, the more likely he is to learn good canine manners.

In order to socialise your Jack Russell effectively, it is helpful to understand how his brain is developing and then you will get a perspective on how he sees the world.

A puppy learns from his mother and from his littermates.

CANINE SOCIALISATION
(Birth to 7 weeks)

This is the time when a dog learns how to be a dog. By interacting with his mother and his littermates, a young pup learns about leadership and submission. He learns to read body posture so that he understands the intentions of his mother and his siblings. A puppy that is taken away from his litter too early may always have behavioural problems with other dogs, either being fearful or aggressive.

SOCIALISATION PERIOD
(7 to 12 weeks)

This is the time to get cracking and introduce your Jack Russell puppy to as many different experiences as possible. This includes meeting different people, other dogs and animals, seeing new sights and hearing a range of sounds, from the vacuum cleaner to the roar of traffic. It may be that your Jack Russell has been reared in kennels and if this is the case, you must work even harder at this stage of his education. A

puppy learns very quickly and what he learns will stay with him for the rest of his life. This is the best time for a puppy to move to a new home, as he is adaptable and ready to form deep bonds.

FEAR-IMPRINT PERIOD
(8 to 11 weeks)

This occurs during the socialisation period and it can be the cause of problems if it is not handled carefully. If a pup is exposed to a frightening or painful experience, it will lead to lasting impressions. Obviously, you will attempt to avoid frightening situations, such as your pup being bullied by a mean-spirited older dog, or a firework going off, but you cannot always protect your puppy from the unexpected. If your pup has a nasty experience, the best plan is to make light of it and distract him by offering him a treat or a game. The pup will take the lead from you and will be reassured that there is nothing to worry about. If you mollycoddle him and sympathise with him, he is far more likely to retain the memory of his fear.

SENIORITY PERIOD
(12 to 16 weeks)

During this period, your Jack Russell puppy starts to cut the apron strings and becomes more independent. He will test out his status to find out who is the pack leader: him or you. Bad habits, such as play biting, which may have been seen as endearing a few weeks earlier, should be firmly discouraged. Remember to use positive, reward-based training, but make sure your puppy knows that you are the leader and must be respected.

SECOND FEAR-IMPRINT PERIOD (6 to 14 months)

This period is not as critical as the first fear-imprint period, but it should still be handled carefully. During this time your Jack Russell may appear apprehensive, or he may show fear of something familiar. You may feel as if you have taken a backwards step, but if you adopt a calm, positive manner, your Jack Russell will see that there is nothing to be frightened of. Do not make your dog confront the thing that frightens him. Simply distract his attention, and give him something else to think about, such as obeying a simple command, such as "Sit" or "Down". This will give you the opportunity to praise and reward your dog and will help to boost his confidence.

As a dog starts to mature he will re-evaluate the world, and may show some fear or apprehension.

YOUNG ADULTHOOD AND MATURITY (1 to 4 years)

The timing of this phase depends on the size of the dog: the bigger the dog, the later it is. This period coincides with a dog's increased size and strength, mental as well as physical. Some dogs, particularly those with a dominant nature, will test your leadership again and may become aggressive towards other dogs. Firmness and continued training are essential at this time, so that your Jack Russell accepts his status in the family pack.

IDEAS FOR SOCIALISATION

When you are socialising your Jack Russell, you want him to experience as many different situations as possible. Try out some of the following ideas, which will ensure your Jack Russell has an all-round education.

If you are taking on a rescued dog and have little knowledge of his background, it is important to work through a programme of socialisation. A young puppy soaks up new experiences like a sponge, but an older dog can still

learn. If a rescued dog shows fear or apprehension, treat him in exactly the same way as you would treat a youngster who is going through the second fear-imprint period.

- Accustom your puppy to household noises, such as the vacuum cleaner, the television and the washing machine.
- Ask visitors to come to the door, wearing different types of clothing – for example, wearing a hat, a long raincoat, or carrying a stick or an umbrella.
- If you do not have children at

Socialising with other dogs is a vital part of your Jack Russell's education.

TRAINING CLUBS

There are lots of training clubs to choose from. Your vet will probably have details of clubs in your area, or you can ask friends who have dogs if they attend a club. Alternatively, use the internet to find out more information. But how do you know if the club is any good?

Before you take your dog, ask if you can go to a class as an observer and find out the following:
• What experience does the instructor(s) have?
• Do they have experience with Jack Russells?
• Is the class well organised and are the dogs reasonably quiet? (A noisy class indicates an unruly atmosphere, which will not be conducive to learning.)
• Are there are a number of classes to suit dogs of different ages and abilities?
• Are positive, reward-based training methods used?
• Does the club train for the Good Citizen Scheme (see page 113)?

If you are not happy with the training club, find another one. An inexperienced instructor who cannot handle a number of dogs in a confined environment can do more harm than good.

home, make sure your Jack Russell has a chance to meet and play with them. Go to a local park and watch children in the play area. You will not be able to take your Jack Russell inside the play area, but he will see children playing and will get used to their shouts of excitement.

- Attend puppy classes. These are designed for puppies between the ages of 12 to 20 weeks and give puppies a chance to play and interact together in a controlled, supervised environment. Your vet will have details of a local class.
- Take a walk around some quiet streets, such as a residential area, so your Jack Russell can get used to the sound of traffic. As he becomes more confident, progress to busier areas. Remember, your lead is like a live wire and your feelings will travel directly to your Jack Russell. Assume a calm, confident manner and your puppy will take the lead from you and have no reason to be fearful.
- Go to a railway station. You don't have to get on a train if you don't need to, but your Jack Russell will have the chance to experience trains, people wheeling luggage, loudspeaker announcements and going up and down stairs and over railway bridges.
- If you live in the town, plan a trip to the country. You can enjoy a day out and provide an opportunity for your Jack

The aim is to own a Jack Russell that is calm and relaxed in all situations.

Russell to see livestock, such as sheep, cattle and horses.

- One of the best places for socialising a dog is at a country fair. There will be crowds of people, livestock in pens, tractors, bouncy castles, fairground rides and food stalls.
- When your dog is over 20 weeks of age, locate a training class for adult dogs. You may find that your local training class has both puppy and adult classes.

THE ADOLESCENT JACK RUSSELL

It happens to every dog – and every owner. One minute you have an obedient well-behaved youngster and the next you have a boisterous adolescent who appears to have forgotten everything he ever learnt.

A Jack Russell male will show adolescent behaviour at any time between 12 months and 18 months; the age this happens often depends on particular bloodlines. In terms of behavioural changes, a male often become more assertive as he pushes the boundaries to see if he can achieve top dog status.

Female Jack Russells may have a first season as early as 6 months of age or as late as 14-15 months. Again, the age this happens often depends on bloodlines as well as individual maturity. An adolescent Jack Russell may become moody as she is coming into season because of hormonal changes, but she rarely shows a major change in personality. However, she also has the urge to elevate her status at this time and she may well take to pleasing herself rather than trying to co-operate with you.

This can be a trying time, but it is important to retain a sense of perspective. Look at the situations from the dog's perspective and respond to uncharacteristic behaviour with firmness and consistency. Just like a teenager, an adolescent Jack Russell feels the need to flex his muscles and challenge the status quo. But if you show that you are a strong leader (see page 90) and are quick to reward good behaviour, your Jack Russell will be happy to accept you as his protector and provider.

An adolescent dog may try to test his boundaries.

WHEN THINGS GO WRONG

Positive, reward-based training has proved to be the most effective method of teaching dogs, but what happens when your Jack Russell does something wrong and you need to show him that his behaviour is unacceptable? The old-fashioned school of dog training used to rely on the powers of punishment and negative reinforcement. A

dog who raided the bin, for example, was smacked. Now we have learnt that it is not only unpleasant and cruel to hit a dog, it is also ineffective. If you hit a dog for stealing, he is more than likely to see you as the bad consequence of stealing, so he may raid the bin again, but probably not when you are around. If he raided the bin some time before you discovered it, he will be even more confused by your punishment, as he will not relate your response to his 'crime'.

A more commonplace example is when a dog fails to respond to a recall in the park. When the dog eventually comes back, the owner puts the dog on the lead

and goes straight home to punish the dog for his poor response. Unfortunately, the dog will have a different interpretation. He does not think: "I won't ignore a recall command because the bad consequence is the end of my play in the park." He thinks: "Coming to my owner resulted in the end of playtime – therefore coming to my owner has a bad consequence, so I won't do that again."

There are a number of strategies to tackle undesirable behaviour – and they have nothing to do with harsh handling.

Ignoring bad behaviour: The Jack Russell is a strong-willed energetic dog and a lot of undesirable behaviour in youngsters is to do with over-exuberance and lack of respect. For example, a young Jack Russell that barks when you are preparing his food, is showing his impatience and is attempting to train you, rather than the other way round. He believes he can change a situation simply by making a noise – and even if he does not get his food any quicker, he is enjoying the attention he is getting when you shout at him to tell him to be quiet. He is still getting attention, so why inhibit his behaviour?

In this situation, the best and most effective response is to ignore your Jack Russell. Suspend food preparations and get on with another task, such as washing up. Do not go near the food or the food bowl again until your Jack Russell is calm and quiet. Repeat this on every occasion when your Jack Russell barks and he will soon learn that barking is non-productive. He is not rewarded with your attention – or with getting food. It will not take long for him to realise that being quiet is the most effective strategy. In this scenario, you have not only taught your Jack Russell to be quiet when you are preparing his food, you have also earned his respect because you have taken control of the situation.

A typical scenario is when a Jack Russell finds an enticing scent and is 'deaf' to your calls.

Stopping bad behaviour: There are occasions when you want to call an instant halt to whatever it is your Jack Russell is doing. He may have just jumped on the sofa, or you may have caught him red-handed in the rubbish bin. He has already committed the 'crime', so your aim is to stop him and to redirect his attention. You can do this by using a deep, firm tone of voice to say "No", which will startle him, and then call him to you in a bright, happy voice. If necessary, you can attract him with a toy or a treat. The moment your Jack Russell stops the undesirable behaviour and comes towards you, you can reward his good behaviour. You can back this up by running through a couple of simple exercises, such as a 'Sit' or a

'Down' and rewarding with treats. In this way, your Jack Russell focuses his attention on you and sees you as the greatest source of reward and pleasure.

In a more extreme situation, when you want to interrupt undesirable behaviour and you know that a simple "No" will not do the trick, you can try something a little more dramatic. If you get a can and fill it with pebbles, it will make a really loud noise when you shake it or throw it. The same effect can be achieved with purpose-made training discs. The dog will be startled and stop what he is doing. Even better, the dog will not associate the unpleasant noise with you. This gives you the perfect opportunity to be the nice guy, calling the dog to you and giving him lots of praise.

PROBLEM BEHAVIOUR

If you have trained your Jack Russell from puppyhood, survived his adolescence and established yourself as a fair and consistent leader, you will end up with a brilliant companion dog. The Jack Russell is a well-balanced dog, who rarely has hang-ups if he has been correctly reared and socialised. Most Jack Russells are out-going, fun-loving and thrive on spending time with their owners. The most common cause of problem behaviour among Jack Russells is boredom. This breed is mentally active and requires mental stimulation. If this is lacking, a Jack Russell will be quick to find his own agenda and will make his life more 'interesting' by becoming destructive or increasingly attention seeking.

It may be that you may have taken on a rescued Jack Russell that has established behavioural problems. If you are worried about your Jack Russell and feel out of your depth, do not delay in seeking professional help. This is readily available, usually through a referral from your vet, or you can find out additional information on the internet (see Appendices for web addresses). An animal behaviourist will have experience in tackling problem behaviour and will be able to help both you and your dog.

Go back to basics and do a simple training exercise so you can reward your Jack Russell for 'good' behaviour.

RESOURCE GUARDING

If you have trained and socialised your Jack Russell correctly, he will know his place in the family pack and will have no desire to challenge your authority. As we have seen, adolescent males may test the boundaries, but this behaviour will not continue if you exhibit the necessary leadership skills.

If you have taken on a rescued dog who has not been trained and socialised, or if you have let your adolescent Jack Russell become over-assertive, you may find you have problems with a dog who is trying to elevate his status.

Assertive behaviour is expressed in many different ways, which may include the following:

- Showing lack of respect for your personal space. For example, your dog will barge through doors ahead of you or jump up at you.
- Ignoring basic obedience commands.
- Showing no respect to younger members of the family, pushing amongst them and completely ignoring them.
- Male dogs may start marking (cocking their leg) in the house.
- Aggression towards people or other dogs (see page 112).

However, the most common behaviour displayed by a Jack Russell who has ideas above his station, is resource guarding. This may take a number of different forms;

- Getting up on to the sofa or your favourite armchair and growling when you tell him to get back on the floor.
- Becoming possessive over a toy, or guarding his food bowl by growling when you get too close.
- Growling when anyone approaches his bed or when anyone gets too close to where he is lying.

In each of these scenarios, the Jack Russell has something he values and he aims to keep it. He does not have sufficient respect for you, his human leader, to give up what he wants and he is 'warning' you to keep away.

If you see signs of your Jack Russell behaving in this way, you must work at lowering his status so that he realises that you are the leader and he must accept your authority. Although you need to be firm, you also need to use positive training methods so that your Jack Russell is rewarded for the behaviour you want. In this way, his 'correct' behaviour will be strengthened and repeated.

The golden rule is not to become confrontational. The dog

LEARNING RESPECT

It is natural for a terrier to want to hold on to something he values.

He needs to learn that *you* own his toys and he must give them up on request.

Job done!

will see this as a challenge and may become even more determined not to co-operate. There are a number of steps you can take to lower your Jack Russell's status which are far more likely to have a successful outcome. They include:

- Go back to basics and hold daily training sessions. Make sure you have some really tasty treats, or find a toy your Jack Russell really values and only bring it out at training sessions. Run through all the training exercises you have taught your Jack Russell. Remember, boredom is very often the key to undesirable behaviour. By giving him things to do, you are giving him mental stimulation and you have the opportunity to make a big fuss of him and reward him when he does well. This will help to reinforce the message that you are the leader and that it is rewarding to do as you ask.
- Teach your Jack Russell something new; this can be as simple as learning a trick, such as shaking paws. Having something new to think about will mentally stimulate your Jack Russell and he will benefit from interacting with you.
- Be 100 per cent consistent

It is good discipline to ask your dog to wait at doorways rather than letting him barge through.

with all house rules – your Jack Russell must never sit on the sofa and you must never allow him to jump up at you.

- If your Jack Russell is becoming possessive over toys, remove all his toys and keep them out of reach. It is then up to you to decide when to produce a toy and to initiate a game. Equally, it is you who will decide when the game is over and when to remove the toy. This teaches your Jack Russell that you 'own' his toys. He has fun playing and interacting with you, but the game is over – and the toy is given up – when you say so.
- If your Jack Russell has been

guarding his food bowl, put the bowl down empty and drop in a little food at a time. Periodically stop dropping in the food and tell your Jack Russell "Sit" and "Wait". Give it a few seconds and then reward him by dropping in more food. This shows your Jack Russell that you are the provider of the food and he can only eat when you allow him to.

- Make sure the family eats before you feed your Jack Russell. Some trainers advocate eating in front of the dog (maybe just a few bites from a biscuit) before starting a training session, so the dog appreciates your elevated status.
- Do not let your Jack Russell Terrier barge through doors ahead of you or leap from the back of the car before you release him. You may need to put your dog on the lead and teach him to "Wait" at doorways and then reward him for letting you go through first.

If your Jack Russell is progressing well with his retraining programme, think about getting involved with a dog sport, such as Agility or Flyball. This will give your Jack Russell a positive outlet for his energies. However, if your Jack Russell is still seeking to be dominant, or you have any other concerns, do not delay in seeking the help of an animal behaviourist.

SEPARATION ANXIETY

A Jack Russell should be brought up to accept short periods of separation from his owner so that he does not become anxious. A new puppy should be left for short periods on his own, ideally in a crate where he cannot get up to any mischief. It is a good idea to leave him with a boredom-busting toy so he will be happily occupied in your absence. When you return, do not rush to the crate and make a huge fuss. Wait a few minutes, and then calmly go to the crate and release your dog, telling him how good he has been. If this scenario is repeated a number of times, your Jack Russell will soon learn that being left on his own is no big deal.

Problems with separation anxiety are most likely to arise if you take on a rescued dog who has major insecurities. You may also find your Jack Russell hates being left if you have failed to accustom him to short periods of isolation when he was growing up. Separation anxiety is expressed in a number of ways and all are equally distressing for both dog and owner. An anxious dog who is left alone may bark and whine continuously, urinate and defecate, and may be extremely destructive.

There are a number of steps you can take when attempting to solve this problem.
- Put up a baby-gate between adjoining rooms and leave your

A boredom busting toy will occupy your dog when he is left alone.

dog in one room while you are in the other room. Your dog will be able to see you and hear you, but he is learning to cope without being right next to you. Build up the amount of time you can leave your dog in easy stages.
- Buy some boredom-busting toys and fill them with some tasty treats. Whenever you leave your dog, give him a food-filled toy so that he is busy while you are away.
- If you have not used a crate before, it is not too late to start. Make sure the crate is cosy and train your Jack Russell to get used to going in his crate while you are in the same room. Gradually build up the amount of time he spends in the crate and then start

leaving the room for short periods. When you return, do not make a fuss of your dog. Leave him for five or ten minutes before releasing him, so that he gets used to your comings and goings.
- Pretend to go out, putting on your coat and jangling keys, but do not leave the house. An anxious dog often becomes hyped up by the ritual of leaving and this will help to desensitize him.
- When you go out, leave a radio or a TV on. Some dogs are comforted by hearing voices and background noise when they are left alone.
- Try to make your absences as short as possible when you are first training your dog to accept being on his own.

Jack Russells who have been well socialised will live in harmony with each other. These brothers are both keen to get the toy – but the smooth coated dog is the boss, and his rough coated brother is prepared to give in to him.

If you take these steps, your dog should become less anxious and over a period of time, you should be able to solve the problem. However, if you are failing to make progress, do not delay in calling in expert help.

AGGRESSION

Aggression is a complex issue, as there are different causes and the behaviour may be triggered by numerous factors. It may be directed towards people, but far more commonly it is directed towards other dogs. Aggression in dogs may be the result of:

- Dominance (see page 108).
- Defensive behaviour: This may be induced by fear, pain or punishment.
- Territory: A dog may become aggressive if strange dogs or people enter his territory (which is generally seen as the house and garden).
- Intra-sexual issues: This is

aggression between sexes – male-to-male or female-to-female.
- Parental instinct: A mother dog may become aggressive if she is protecting her puppies.

The Jack Russell has the reputation for being a feisty breed who does not always get on well with other dogs. However, it is worth remembering that this was a breed that was developed specifically to work in packs. Therefore, there is no reason why a Jack Russell should be aggressive. Certainly, a dog who has been well socialised has been given sufficient exposure to other dogs at significant stages of his development will stand a far better chance of interacting peacefully.

However, you may have taken on an older, rescued dog that

has been poorly socialised and there is something in his history that has made him aggressive. Or you may have a dog who has become dominant in his own home and family and so he is assertive in his dealings with other dogs, as he believes he is top dog.

If dominance is the underlying cause, you can try the measures outlined in this chapter. Equally if your dog has been poorly socialised, you can try to make up for lost time and work with other dogs of sound temperament in controlled situations. But if you are concerned about your dog's behaviour, you would be well advised to call in professional help. If the aggression is directed towards people, you should seek immediate advice. This behaviour can escalate very quickly and could lead to disastrous consequences.

NEW CHALLENGES

If you enjoy training your Jack Russell you may want to try one of the many dog sports that are now on offer.

GOOD CITIZEN SCHEME

This is a scheme run by the Kennel Club in the UK and the American Kennel Club in the USA. The schemes promote responsible ownership and help you to train a well-behaved dog who will fit in with the community. The schemes are excellent for all pet owners and they are also a good starting point if you plan to compete with your Jack Russell when he is older. The KC and the AKC schemes vary in format. In the UK there are three levels: bronze, silver and gold, with each test becoming progressively more demanding. In the AKC scheme there is a single test.

Some of the exercises include:
- Walking on a loose lead among people and other dogs.
- Recall amid distractions.
- A controlled greeting where dogs stay under control while their owners meet.
- The dog allows all-over grooming and handling by his owner, and also accepts being handled by the examiner.
- Stays, with the owner in sight and then out of sight.
- Food manners, allowing the owner to eat without begging and taking a treat on command.
- Sendaway – sending the dog to his bed.

The Parson Russell Terrier is recognised by the Kennel Club and can compete in all KC shows.

The tests are designed to show the control you have over your dog and his ability to respond correctly and remain calm in all situations. The Good Citizen Scheme is taught at most training clubs. For more information, log on to the Kennel Club or AKC website (see Appendices).

SHOWING

The Jack Russell is not recognised by the Kennel Club, so showing opportunities are limited. For information, you will need to contact one of the Jack Russell breed clubs. If you want to get involved with the show world, the best plan is to find out about Parson Russell Terriers and decide whether you want to acquire this breed, which is closely related to the Jack Russell and is recognised by the Kennel Club.

Many training clubs hold ringcraft classes, which are run by experienced showgoers. At these classes, you will learn how to handle your dog in the ring and you will also find out about rules, procedures and show ring etiquette.

The best plan is to start off at some small, informal shows where you can practise and learn the tricks of the trade before graduating to bigger shows.

COMPETING IN AGILITY

With training the Jack Russell can become highly motivated
and compete successfully at the top level.

Powering through the tunnel and over a jump.

COMPETITIVE OBEDIENCE

Dogs do not have to be registered with the English Kennel Club to take part in competitive obedience, so this is another avenue open to the Jack Russell. There are various levels of achievement, starting with Beginners, but this is highly competitive, even at the lower levels. Marks are lost for even the slightest crooked angle noticed when the dog is sitting and if a dog has a momentary attention deficit or works too far away from his owner in heelwork, again points will be deducted.

Nonetheless, many Jack Russell owners enjoy this challenge and many a terrier has worked his way up through the classes, even to Championship level. Competition is open to dogs from the age of six months. The exercises that must be mastered include the following:

- **Heelwork:** Dog and handler must complete a set pattern on and off the lead, which includes left turns, right turns, about turns and changes of pace.
- **Recall:** This may be when the handler is stationary or on the move.
- **Retrieve:** This may be a dumbbell or any article chosen by the judge.
- **Sendaway:** The dog is sent to a designated spot and must go into an instant 'Down' until he is recalled by the handler.
- **Stays:** The dog must stay in the 'Sit' and in the 'Down' for a set amount of time. In advanced classes, the handler is out of sight.
- **Scent:** The dog must retrieve a single cloth from a pre-arranged pattern of cloths that has his owner's scent, or in

Negotiating the weaves.

Running down the A frame

advanced classes, the judge's scent. There may also be decoy cloths.

- **Distance control.** The dog must execute a series of moves ('Sit', 'Stand', 'Down') without moving from his position and with the handler at a distance.

Even though competitive obedience requires accuracy and precision, make sure you make it fun for your Jack Russell, with lots of praise and rewards so that you motivate him to do his best. Many training clubs run

advanced classes for those who want to compete in obedience, or you can hire the services of a professional trainer for one-on-one sessions.

AGILITY

This fun sport has grown enormously in popularity over the past few years, and the quick-witted, fast moving Jack Russell has achieved a high degree of success. If you fancy having a go, make sure you have good control over your Jack Russell and keep him slim. Agility is a very physical sport,

which demands fitness from both dog and handler.

In agility competitions, each dog must complete a set course over a series of obstacles which include:

- Jumps (upright hurdles and long jump, varying in height – small, medium and large, depending on the size of the dog)
- Weaves
- A-frame
- Dog walk
- Seesaw
- Tunnels (collapsible and rigid)
- Tyre

If you do not want to get involved in competition, take time to teach your Jack Russell some fun tricks – he will be only too happy to show off when friends come round!

dog, who may suffer injury if he puts strain on bones and joints while he is still growing.

WORKING TRIALS

Working trials in Britain have been around for many years and the trial calendar can be very crowded, especially in spring and autumn. Although historically larger dogs, such as German Shepherd Dogs were used in working trials, things have changed over the years and now they are open to any dog that can be suitably trained. Added to this they do not need to be registered with the English Kennel Club, which make Jack Russells suitable participants. There is however, a minimum age for competition, which is 18 months.

Competition at working trials is fierce and qualification is by no means easy. The Jack Russell's excellent nose makes him a strong contender for track and search, and this agile little fellow works well in the agility section too. But because they are such live-wires, they can be more difficult to control than many other breeds. They lack the concentration of some of the more easily trained breeds and require a substantial amount of motivation. 'Stays', in particular, they often find rather difficult, as Jack Russells always seem ready for the off and for a new adventure!

In training a Jack Russell, little and often seems generally to be the best criteria to follow. Also owners should bear in mind that dependent upon both the season

Dogs may compete in Jumping classes, with jumps, tunnels and weaves, or in Agility classes, which have the full set of equipment. Faults are awarded for poles down on the jumps, missed contact points on the A-frame, dog walk and seesaw and refusals. If a dog takes the wrong course, he is eliminated. The winner is the dog that completes the course in the fastest time with no faults. As you progress up the levels, courses become progressively harder with more twists, turns and changes of direction.

If you want to get involved in Agility, you will need to find a club that specialises in the sport (see Appendices). You will not be allowed to start training until your Jack Russell is 12 months old and you cannot compete until he is 18 months old. This rule is for the protection of the

DANCING WITH DOGS

This sport is relatively new, but it is becoming increasingly popular. It is very entertaining to watch, but it is certainly not as simple as it looks. To perform a choreographed routine to music with your Jack Russell demands a huge amount of training.

Dancing with dogs is divided into two categories: Heelwork to Music and Canine Freestyle. In Heelwork to Music, the dog must work closely with his handler and show a variety of close 'heelwork' positions. In Canine Freestyle, the routine can be more flamboyant, with the dog working at a distance from the handler and performing spectacular tricks. Routines are judged on style and presentation, content and accuracy.

and location, the ground used for tracking varies.

There are three basic components involved in Working Trials:

- **Control:** Dog and handler must complete obedience exercises, but the work does not have to be as precise as it is in competitive obedience.
- **Agility:** In Companion Dog (CD) and Utility Dog (UD) the jumps for dogs under 15 inches (38 cm), which should include all Jack Russells, are a 2 ft (0.60 m) hurdle, a 6 ft (1.82 m) long jump and a 4 ft (1.22 m) scale.
- **Nosework:** The dog must follow a track that has been laid over a set course. The surface may vary and the length of time between the track being laid and the dog starting work is increased in the advanced classes.

The ladder of stakes are: Companion Dog, Utility Dog, Working Dog, Tracking Dog and Patrol Dog. However, the heights of jumps are not reduced after Utility Dog stakes so Jack Russells cannot compete in the higher stakes. In the US, tracking is a sport in its own right and is very popular among Jack Russell owners.

If you want to get involved in Working Trials, you will need to find a specialist club or a trainer that specialises in the sport. For more information, see Appendices.

FLYBALL

The Jack Russell is not a natural retriever, but many enjoy the hurly burly and excitement of competing in Flyball. Flyball is a team sport; the dogs love it and it is undoubtedly the noisiest of all the canine sports!

Four dogs are selected to run in a relay race against an opposing team. The dogs are sent out by their handlers to jump four hurdles, catch the ball from the flyball box and then return over the hurdles. At the top level, this sport is fast and furious and although it is dominated by Border Collies, the Jack Russell can make a big contribution. This is particularly true in multibreed competitions, where the team is made up of four dogs of different breeds and only one can be a Border Collie or a Working Sheepdog. Points are awarded to dogs and teams. Annual awards are given to top dogs and top teams, and milestone awards are given out to dogs as they attain points throughout their flyballing careers.

SUMMING UP

The Jack Russell is an outstanding companion dog in the world – and once you have owned one, no other breed will do. He is intelligent, fun-loving, feisty and loyal. Make sure you keep your half of the bargain: spend time socialising and training your Jack Russell so that you can be proud to take him anywhere and he will always be a credit to you.

THE PERFECT JACK RUSSELL

Chapter 7

I n Britain every breed of dog has a Breed Standard, which gives breeders a guideline to follow so that the puppies they produce look like that particular breed, rather than another one. Most Breed Standards are drawn up by the Kennel Club, but others are not, such as those of various working terriers, including the Jack Russell, Lucas Terrier and Patterdale. In these cases the Standards are compiled by the breed clubs and sometimes by experienced breed enthusiasts.

A Breed Standard is effectively a picture painted in words. However, each person's interpretation of the Standard is slightly different, otherwise at conformation shows the same dog would always win.

Having said that, some things within each standard are not open to interpretation, such as

colour, size and carriage of ear. We are told, for example, that a Jack Russell's hindquarters should be 'strong and muscular', so if they were weak and wobbly this would not be characteristic of the breed. Equally this is a predominantly white dog, so if it were almost totally black with a just a white spot over one eye, it would certainly not be a typical Jack Russell!

Although there are many similarities between the Jack Russell and the Parson Russell Terriers, there are also many differences too. The differences though, are more noticeable in some countries than in others, because of the way the two breeds have been linked up and divided, and according to their respective Breed Standards.

In this chapter you will find it interesting to compare the two

Standards in use in Britain. As the Jack Russell is not a Kennel Club registered breed, the Standard is issued by the Jack Russell Terrier Club of Great Britain (JRTCGB). The Standard for the Parson Russell Terrier is issued by the Kennel Club.

But before we look at either, it may be prudent to consider and inwardly digest the Breed Standard written up in 1904 by Arthur Heinemann, the journalist and hunting man who, following the death of Reverend John Russell, formed the Devon and Somerset Badger Club. This Standard is given on page 120.

THE JACK RUSSELL TERRIER CLUB BREED STANDARD
Established in 1974 and a member of the National Working Terrier Federation, the Jack Russell Terrier Club of GB

THE 1904 BREED STANDARD

HEAD

The skull should be flat, moderately broad, gradually decreasing to the eyes. Little stop should be apparent. The cheeks must not be full. Ears V-shaped and small, of moderate thickness and dropping forward close to the cheek, not by the side. Upper and lower jaws strong and muscular and of fair punishing strength. Not much falling away below the eyes. The nose should be black. The eyes dark, small, and deep set, full of fire, life and intelligence, and circular in shape. Teeth level, i.e. upper on the outside of the lower.

NECK

Clean and muscular of fair length gradually widening to shoulders.

SHOULDERS

Long and sloping, well laid-back, fine at points, clearly cut at withers.

CHEST

Deep but not broad.

BACK

Powerful, very slightly arched, fore ribs moderately arched, back ribs deep. The terrier should be well ribbed up.

HINDQUARTERS

Strong and muscular, free from droop, thighs long and powerful, hocks near the ground, dog standing well on them. Not straight in the stifle.

(JRTCGB) drew up the following Breed Standard, with the additional clause that a Jack Russell Terrier should not show any strong characteristics of any other breed.

CHARACTERISTICS

The terrier must present a lively, active and alert appearance. It should impress with its fearless and happy disposition. It should be remembered that the Jack Russell is a working terrier and should retain these instincts. Nervousness, cowardice and over-aggression should be discouraged, and it should always appear confident.

GENERAL APPEARANCE

A sturdy, tough terrier, very much on its toes all the time, measuring between 10 ins and 15 ins at the withers. The body length must be in proportion to the height, and it should present a compact, balanced image, always being in solid, hard condition.

HEAD

Should be well balanced and in proportion to the body. The skull should be flat, of moderate width at the ears, narrowing to the eyes. There should be a defined stop but not over-pronounced. The length of muzzle from the nose to the stop should be slightly shorter than the distance from the stop to the occiput. The nose should be black. The jaw should be powerful and well boned with strongly muscled cheeks.

EYES

Should be almond shaped, dark

STERN

Set on high, carried gaily but never over the back or curled. Of good strength and length. A 'pipe cleaning' tail, or too short, is most objectionable.

LEGS

Perfectly straight, showing no ankle in front. Strong in bone throughout, short and straight to the pastern. Fore and back legs carried straight forward when travelling, stifles not turned outward. Elbows should hang perpendicular to the body, working free to the side.

FEET

Round, compact, not large, soles hard and tough, toes moderately arched, turned neither in nor out.

COAT

Dense, a trifle wiry, abundant. Belly and undersides not bare.

COLOUR

White, with acceptable tan, grey or black at head and root of tail. Brindle or liver markings are objectionable.

SYMMETRY, SIZE AND CHARACTER

Terrier must present a gay, lively and active appearance. Bone and strength in a small compass are essentials, but not cloggy or coarse. Speed and endurance must be apparent. Not too short or too long in leg. Fourteen inches at the withers ideal for a dog, thirteen for a bitch. Weight when in working condition about fourteen pounds, but a pound more or less entirely acceptable. Conformation that of an adult vixen.

DISQUALIFYING POINTS

Too short, too leggy, legs not straight. Nose white, cherry or spotted considerably with these colours. Ears prick or rose. Mouth under or over shot. Excessively nervous or savage.

in colour and full of life and intelligence.

EARS

Small 'V' shaped drop ears carried forward close to the head and of moderate thickness.

MOUTH

Strong teeth with the top slightly overlapping the lower.

NECK

Clean and muscular, of good length, gradually widening at the shoulders.

The head is moderately wide, narrowing towards the almond-shaped eyes.

The drop ears are small and 'V-shaped'.

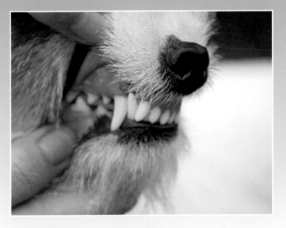

The teeth meet in a cissor bite, with the teeth in the upper jaw closely overlapping the teeth in the lower.

FOREQUARTERS

The shoulders should be sloping and well laid back, fine at points and clearly cut at the withers. Forelegs should be strong and straight boned with joints in correct alignment. Elbows hanging perpendicular to the body and working free of the sides.

BODY

The chest should be shallow, narrow and the front legs set not too widely apart, giving an athletic, rather than heavily chested appearance. As a guide only, the chest should be small enough to be easily spanned behind the shoulders, by average hands, when the terrier is in a fit, working condition. The back should be strong, straight and, in comparison to the height of the terrier, give a balanced image. The loin should be slightly arched.

HINDQUARTERS

Should be strong and muscular, well put together with good angulations and bend of stifle, giving plenty of drive and propulsion. Looking from behind, hocks must be straight.

FEET

Round, hard-padded, of cat-like appearance, neither turning in nor out.

TAIL

Should be set rather high, carried gaily and in proportion to body length, usually about four inches long, providing a good hand-hold.

COAT

Smooth, without being so sparse as not to provide a certain amount of protection from the elements and undergrowth. Rough or broken coated, without being woolly.

COLOUR

White should predominate with tan, black, or brown markings. Brindle markings are unacceptable.

GAIT

Movement should be free, lively, well co-ordinated with straight action in front and behind.

PLEASE NOTE:

1) Dogs and bitches should be entire and capable of breeding. Dogs should be shown to have both testicles fully descended into the scrotum.
2) Old scars or injuries, the result of work or accident, should not be allowed to prejudice the terrier's chance in the show ring unless they interfere with its movement or with its utility for work or stud.

3) For showing purposes, terriers are classified into two groups according to their height, which are 10-12 ins and over 12-15 ins.

INTERPRETATION AND ANALYSIS

STRUCTURE AND ANATOMY

A Jack Russell Terrier was intended to follow quarry underground, so his chest and ribbing is a determining factor as to whether this is possible. However determined a terrier, if he is too large he is not fit for purpose. Perhaps of surprise to those who are not involved with hunting, the fox is more finely structured than a Jack Russell, in addition to which it has a loose-fitting pelt which allows flexibility. The fox is an incredibly clever animal and a terrier needs to be structured such that he can cope competently with the fox's cunning ways.

The Jack Russell's small 'V' shaped ears should bend in the middle, folding forward to the front of the head. The teeth are only mentioned briefly in the above Standard, but this breed should have a scissor bite, meaning that the upper incisors closely overlap the lower ones, a very efficient dental formation. All teeth should be relatively sharp.

Quite a lot of Jack Russells are seen with bowed forelegs, but this is incorrect and is contrary to the Breed Standard. Such legs are often known as 'benched' legs and are a sign of achrondoplasia, which is a misalignment of bones

The Jack Russell should have a smooth outline and strong, sturdy limbs.

and joints. A high proportion of Jack Russells thus affected will not have any problem as a result, but some get progressively worse causing a dog to become crippled later in life.

GENERAL OUTLINE

Whatever the coat type, the Jack Russell's outline should be clean and easy to identify. This goes back to Reverend John Russell's original requirements for the breed, that all terriers should look smooth from shooting distance, whatever type of coat they had.

Although the broken and rough coated terriers have a generally more ragged outline, especially around the neck and shoulders, the outline is well defined on all other parts of the anatomy. Legs are clean and smooth, although they have thick, short, protective hair, and it is important that the belly and undersides are well covered.

A WORD ABOUT COAT

Jack Russell Terriers have three different coat types: smooth, broken-coated and rough, all of which are equally acceptable, provided they are good quality both in depth and texture. We must always bear in mind that for any dog that was bred to work, coat is a very important factor in his survival and success in the field. All three Jack Russell coat types should be weatherproof and suitable to offer protection, not only from the cold and wet, but also from injury.

Each of the three coats has a dense undercoat and weatherproof topcoat, the difference being in the length of the topcoat, which is actually made up of guard hairs. It is the length of these hairs that give quite a different look to Jack Russells that are essentially the same in type; if you were able to take the very same dog and put

COLOUR

On the Jack Russell Terrier, blue or chocolate patches on the coat, or indeed, on the nose, are highly undesirable features. When puppies with these colours are born, it is strongly recommended that neither parent should be used in a future breeding programme.

The white and lemon Jack Russell is really just a lighter version of the white and tan. Such puppies are usually born white, the coloured areas developing over the first couple of weeks of their life. The tan colour varies quite considerably and although it may appear the same when viewed from a distance, it may even be sable or grizzle.

On the other hand, puppies that are white and tan are actually born with their tan patches, which only rarely change colour. Patches that will become sable or grizzle are usually black when the puppy is born, but this turns to its eventual colour over the course of a week or so.

Tricoloured Jack Russells are different again. Most, when born, appear black and white, with just a touch of tan colouring around the eyes and on the cheeks. The tan colouring develops further as the puppies grow. Less common are white Jack Russells with black markings, but those which have tan spots above the eyes and on the cheeks, as well as inside the ears and on the underside of the tail, are found a little more often.

A Jack Russell's lips and eye rims should be darkly pigmented. Some puppies are actually born with a black mask, but this fades with maturity, just a little black remaining at the corners of the mouth and around the eyes.

In following the background history of individual Jack Russells, the colour of the patches will indicate breeds that may have been involved in its make-up. But breeds that have been crossed with Jack Russells all bring in different characteristics that are considered undesirable, largely because they affect the work the breed was designed to do.

Before moving to the Parson Russell Terrier's Breed Standard, some readers may be interested to read the Jack Russell's FCI Standard, as it contains rather more detail than our own.

Jack Russells are typically white and tan, though the shade can vary considerably and is often an indication of the breeds involved in the dog's ancestry.

on it all three types of coat, it would, to the eye at least, look very different.

The undercoat is dense and soft, so acts as good insulation. Topcoat is hard, not harsh, straight and oily, making this a waterproof outer layer. Length of the topcoat varies from as little as 2 cms (0.5 ins) to 6 cms (2.5 ins) and is more especially long around the neck and shoulders. Even in the smooth coated Jack Russell, the coat tends to be longer here. It is clear that in working terriers, a dog with an open or thin coat is less able to withstand the elements and is more prone to injury. Without his waterproof coat, a Jack Russell would stand a much greater chance of suffering from stiff joints, especially in old age.

Another reason for the practical coat is that it offers protection against the foe when working underground; indeed this is common to many working breeds, not just Jack Russells.

JACK RUSSELL TERRIER: THE FCI STANDARD

ORIGIN
England.

COUNTRY OF DEVELOPMENT
Australia.

DATE OF PUBLICATION OF THE ORIGINAL VALID STANDARD
25.10.2000.

The Jack Russell has a keen expression and a bold, friendly temperament.

UTILIZATION
A good working Terrier with ability to go to ground. An excellent companion dog.

CLASSIFICATION F.C.I.
Group 3 Terriers. Section 2 Small Terriers. With working trial.

BRIEF HISTORICAL SUMMARY
The Jack Russell originated in England in the 1800s due to the efforts of the Reverend John Russell. He developed a strain of Fox Terriers to suit his needs for a dog to run with his foxhounds and go to ground to bolt the fox and other quarry from their dens. Two varieties evolved with basically similar Standards except for differences, mainly in height and proportions. The taller, more squarely built dog is now known as the Parson Russell Terrier and the shorter, slightly longer proportioned dog, is known as the Jack Russell Terrier.

GENERAL APPEARANCE
A strong, active, lithe working Terrier of great character with flexible body of medium length. His smart movement matches his keen expression. Tail docking is optional and the coat may be smooth, rough or broken.

IMPORTANT PROPORTIONS
• The overall dog is longer than high.
• The depth of the body from the withers to the brisket should equal the length of foreleg from elbows to the ground.
• The girth behind the elbows should be about 40 to 43 cm.

BEHAVIOUR/TEMPERAMENT
A lively, alert and active Terrier with a keen, intelligent expression. Bold and fearless, friendly but quietly confident.

HEAD

CRANIAL REGION
Skull: The skull should be flat and of moderate width gradually decreasing in width to the eyes and tapering to a wide muzzle.
Stop: Well defined but not over pronounced.

FACIAL REGION
Nose: Black.
Muzzle: The length from the stop to the nose should be slightly shorter than from the

JACK RUSSELL TERRIER

AN INTERNATIONAL BREED

The immensely popular Jack Russell has a strong presence in many countries of the world, including America and Australia.

The Jack Russell Terrier Club of Great Britain hosts an annual show for the best Jack Russells in the country. The standard is extremely high and draws many entrants and spectators. Featured here are two top Jack Russells from the 2006 National, judged by Mrs Lynn Clough: Best in Show (left) Bicester Tag and Reserve Brockton Jock.

UNJ CH Saltisgarden Good Times, CGC (Viking). Bred by Ingrid & Henrik Saltzman (Saltisgarden Jack Russells, Sweden) and owned and handled by Eva & Cathy Jo Long (Turning Leaf Jack Russells). This truly international dog was the number 8 UKC Jack Russell Terrier for 2008 with the United Kennel Club and is also registered with the FCI, AKC and FSS. He has multiple Best of Breed and Group wins under his belt and also competes in Earthwork and Terrier Racing.

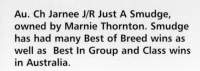

Au. Ch Jarnee J/R Just A Smudge, owned by Marnie Thornton. Smudge has had many Best of Breed wins as well as Best In Group and Class wins in Australia.

stop to the occiput.

Lips: Tight-fitting and pigmented black.

Jaws/Teeth: Very strong, deep, wide and powerful. Strong teeth closing to a scissor bite.

Eyes: Small dark and with keen expression. MUST not be prominent and eyelids should fit closely. The eyelid rims should be pigmented black. Almond shape.

Ears: Button or dropped of good texture and great mobility.

Cheeks: The cheek muscles should be well developed.

NECK

Strong and clean allowing head to be carried with poise.

BODY

General: Rectangular.

Back: Level. The length from the withers to the root of tail slightly greater than the height from the withers to the ground.

Loin: The loins should be short, strong and deeply muscled.

Chest: Chest deep rather than wide, with good clearance from the ground, enabling the brisket to be located at the height mid-way between the ground and the withers. Ribs should be well sprung from the spine, flattening on the sides so that the girth behind the elbows can be spanned by two hands - about 40 cm to 43 cm.

Sternum: Point of sternum clearly in front of the point of shoulder.

TAIL

May droop at rest. When moving should be erect and if docked the tip should be on the same level as ears.

FOREQUARTERS

Shoulders: Well sloped back and not heavily loaded with muscle.

Upper arm: Of sufficient length and angulation to ensure elbows are set under the body.

Forelegs: Straight in bone from the elbows to the toes whether viewed from the front or the side.

HINDQUARTERS

Strong and muscular, balanced in proportion to the shoulder.

Stifles: Well angulated.

Hock joints: Low set.

Rear pastern (Metatarsus): Parallel when viewed from behind while in free standing position.

FEET

Round, hard, padded, not large, toes moderately arched, turned neither in nor out.

GAIT / MOVEMENT

True, free and springy.

COAT

May be smooth, broken or rough. Must be weatherproof. Coats should not be altered (stripped out) to appear smooth or broken.

COLOUR

White MUST predominate with black and/or tan markings. The tan markings can be from the lightest tan to the richest tan (chestnut).

SIZE AND WEIGHT

Ideal Height: 25 cm (10 ins) to 30 cm (12 ins).

Weight: Being the equivalent of 1 kg to each 5 cm in height, i.e. a 25 cm high dog should weigh approximately 5 kg and a 30 cm high dog should weigh 6 kg.

FAULTS

Any departure from the foregoing points should be considered a fault and the seriousness with which the fault should be regarded should be in exact proportion to its degree, and its effect upon the health and welfare of the dog. However, the following weaknesses should be particularly penalised:
- Lack of true Terrier characteristics.
- Lack of balance, i.e. over exaggeration of any points.
- Sluggish or unsound movement.
- Faulty mouth.

Any dog clearly showing physical or behavioural abnormalities shall be disqualified.

N.B. Male animals should have two apparently normal testicles fully descended into the scrotum.

A LITTLE PARSON RUSELL HISTORY

Earlier you read Arthur Heinemann's 1904 Breed Standard. This was used by the Devon and Somerset Badger Club, the name of which was later changed to the Parson Jack Russell Terrier Club. It was registered with the Kennel Club as one of 28 clubs affiliated to the Fox Terrier Club.

Heinemann died in 1930, but the club was continued, headed by Mrs Harris who had been Heinemann's kennelmaid. Unfortunately the club eventually folded, shortly before the Second World War. But following the war, as we know, there was a resurgence in interest in small hunt terriers who were mainly white in colour and in other cross-bred terriers, all of which were known loosely as Jack Russells.

It was in the autumn of 1983 that Parson Russell enthusiasts became concerned that what they considered to be the type of terrier most closely associated with Reverend Russell might become extinct, or just an unrecognised 'mongrel'. In consequence they re-formed the Parson Jack Russell Terrier Club (PJRT Club) and adopted the Standard which had been drawn up by Heinemann in 1904. Although they made application to the Kennel Club for registration soon afterwards, this was not approved.

This was the first of several applications that were made to the Kennel Club, but always they fell on stony ground. Subsequently they changed the format of the Breed Standard to fall in line with those already issued by the KC and it became necessary to substantiate

The Parson presents an overall picture of balance and flexibility.

pedigrees for each terrier on the Foundation Register. Finally, on January 9th 1990, the Kennel Club approved the Parson Jack Russell Terrier, as a variant of the Fox Terrier.

In 1999 the Kennel Club acted on several requests made by members of the PJRT Club and agreed to change the name of the breed to Parson Russell Terrier, so accordingly the name of the club changed too. According to the club, this is the traditional West Country name for this terrier "and highlights the difference between the 19th century foxing terriers and the so-called Jack Russell".

THE KC PARSON RUSSELL TERRIER BREED STANDARD

The following Breed Standard is the one that is approved by the English Kennel Club:

GENERAL APPEARANCE
Workmanlike, active and agile; built for speed and endurance. Overall picture of balance and flexibility. Honourable scars permissible.

CHARACTERISTICS
Essentially a working terrier with ability and conformation to go to ground and run with hounds.

TEMPERAMENT
Bold and friendly.

HEAD AND SKULL
Flat, moderately broad, gradually narrowing to the eyes. Shallow stop. Length from nose to stop slightly shorter than from stop to occiput. Nose black.

EYES
Almond-shaped, fairly deep-set, dark, keen expression.

EARS
Small, V-shaped, dropping forward, carried close to head, tip of ear to reach corner of eye, fold not to appear above top of skull. Leather of moderate thickness.

MOUTH
Jaws strong, muscular. Teeth with a perfect, regular and

complete scissor bite, i.e. upper teeth closely overlapping lower teeth and set square to the jaws.

NECK
Clean, muscular, of good length, gradually widening to shoulders.

FOREQUARTERS
Shoulders long and sloping, well laid back, cleanly cut at withers. Legs strong, must be straight with joints turning neither in nor out. Elbows close to body, working free of the sides.

BODY
Ribs not over-sprung. Chest of moderate depth, not to come below point of elbow, capable of being spanned behind the shoulders by average size hands. Back strong and straight. Loin slightly arched. Well balanced. Overall length slightly longer than height from withers to ground.

HINDQUARTERS
Strong, muscular with good angulation and bend of stifle. Hocks set low and rear pasterns parallel giving plenty of drive.

FEET
Compact with firm pads, turning neither in nor out.

The Parson may be smooth-coated (front) or rough-coated (rear).

TAIL
Previously customarily docked. *Docked:* Length complimenting the body while providing a good handhold. Strong, straight, moderately high set, carried well up on the move. *Undocked:* Of moderate length and as straight as possible, giving a general balance to the dog, thick at the root and tapering towards the end. Moderately high set, carried well up on the move.

GAIT/MOVEMENT
Free-striding, well co-ordinated; straight action front and behind.

COAT
Naturally harsh, close and dense, whether rough or smooth. Belly and undersides coated. Skin must be thick and loose.

COLOUR
Entirely white or predominantly white with tan, lemon or black markings, or any combination of these colours, preferably confined to the head and/or root of tail.

SIZE
Most importantly a working terrier should be capable of being spanned behind the shoulders by average sized hands. Ideal height at withers: dogs 36 cms (14 ins.), bitches 33 cms (13 ins.) It is recognised that smaller terriers are required for work in certain areas and lower heights are therefore quite acceptable provided that soundness and balance are maintained.

FAULTS
Any departure from the foregoing points should be considered a fault and the seriousness with which the fault should be regarded should be in exact proportion to its degree and its effect upon the health and welfare of the dog. Male animals should have two apparently normal testicles fully descended into the scrotum.

HAPPY AND HEALTHY

Chapter 8

The Jack Russell Terrier and his close cousin, the Parson Russell Terrier, are stoical dogs with a life-span which can run well into double figures. Although he has many of the terrier traits one would expect, the Jack Russell is renowned as a plucky, faithful companion and a willing friend on a non-conditional basis. He will, however, of necessity rely on you for food and shelter, accident prevention and medication. A healthy Jack Russell is a happy chap, looking to please and amuse his owner.

There are a few genetic conditions recognised in the Jack Russell, which will be covered later in the chapter (see page 144).

ROUTINE HEALTH CARE

VACCINATION

There is much debate over the issue of vaccination at the moment. The timing of the final part of the initial vaccination course for a puppy and the frequency of subsequent booster vaccinations, are both under scrutiny. An evaluation of the relative risk for each disease plays a part, depending on the local situation.

Many owners think that the actual vaccination is the protection, so that their puppy can go out for walks as soon as he has had the final part of the puppy vaccination course. This is not the case. The rationale behind vaccination is to stimulate the immune system into producing protective antibodies, which will be triggered if the patient is subsequently exposed to that particular disease. This means that a further one or two weeks will have to pass before an effective level of protection will have developed.

Vaccines against viruses stimulate longer-lasting protection than those against bacteria, whose effect may only persist for a matter of months in some cases. There is also the possibility of an individual failing to mount a full immune response to a vaccination: although the vaccine schedule may have been followed as recommended, that particular dog remains vulnerable.

An individual dog's level of protection against rabies, as demonstrated by the antibody titre in a blood sample, is routinely tested in the UK in order to fulfil the requirements of the Pet Travel Scheme (PETS). This is not required at the current time with other individual diseases in order to gauge the need for booster vaccination or to determine the effect of a course of vaccines. Instead, your veterinary surgeon will advise a protocol based upon the vaccines

When you take your Jack Russell for his booster, the vet can give him a general check-up.

available, local disease prevalence and the lifestyle of you and your dog.

It is worth remembering that maintaining a fully effective level of immune protection against the diseases appropriate to your locale is vital. These are serious diseases which may result in the death of your dog and some may have the potential to be passed on to his human family (so-called zoonotic potential for transmission). This is where you will be grateful for your veterinary surgeon's own knowledge and advice.

The American Animal Hospital Association laid down guidance at the end of 2006 for the vaccination of dogs in North America. Core diseases were defined as distemper, adenovirus, parvovirus and rabies. So-called non-core diseases are kennel cough, Lyme disease and leptospirosis. A decision to

vaccinate against one or more non-core diseases will be based on an individual's level of risk, determined on life-style and where you live in the US.

Do remember, however, that the booster visit to the veterinary surgery is not 'just' for a booster. I am regularly correcting my clients when they announce that they have 'just' brought their pet for a booster. Instead, this appointment is a chance for a full health check and evaluation of how a particular dog is doing. After all, we are all conversant with the adage that a human year is equivalent to seven canine years.

There have been attempts in recent times to re-set the scale for two reasons: small breeds live longer than giant breeds, and dogs are generally living longer than previously. I have seen dogs of 17 and 18 years of age but to

say a dog is 119 or 126 years old is plainly meaningless. It does emphasise the fact, though, that a dog's health can change dramatically over the course of a single year, because dogs age at a far greater rate than humans.

For me as a veterinary surgeon, the booster vaccination visit is a challenge: how much can I find of which the owner was unaware, such as rotten teeth or a heart murmur? Even monitoring bodyweight year upon year is of use, because bodyweight can creep up, or down, without an owner realising. Being overweight is unhealthy, but it may take an outsider's remark to make an owner realise that there is a problem. Conversely, a drop in bodyweight may be the only pointer to an underlying problem.

The diseases against which dogs are vaccinated include:

Kennel Cough spreads rapidly among dogs that live together.

ADENOVIRUS

Canine Adenovirus 1 (CAV-1) affects the liver (hepatitis) and causes the classic 'blue eye' appearance in some affected dogs, whilst CAV-2 is a cause of kennel cough (see later). Vaccines often include both canine adenoviruses.

DISTEMPER

This disease is sometimes called 'hardpad' from the characteristic changes to the pads of the paws. It has a worldwide distribution, but fortunately vaccination has been very effective at reducing its occurrence. It is caused by a virus and affects the respiratory, gastro-intestinal (gut) and nervous systems, so it causes a wide range of illnesses. Fox and urban stray dog populations are most at risk, and therefore responsible for local outbreaks.

KENNEL COUGH

Also known as infectious tracheobronchitis. *Bordetella bronchiseptica* is not only a major cause of kennel cough but also a common secondary infection on top of another cause. Being a bacterium, it is susceptible to treatment with appropriate antibiotics, but the immunity stimulated by the vaccine is therefore short-lived (six to twelve months).

This vaccine is often in a form to be administered down the nostrils in order to stimulate local immunity at the point of entry, so to speak. Do not be alarmed to see your veterinary surgeon using needle and syringe to draw up the vaccine, because the needle will be replaced with a special plastic introducer, allowing the vaccine to be gently instilled into each nostril. Dogs generally resent being held more

than the actual intra-nasal vaccine, and I have learnt that covering the patient's eyes helps greatly.

Kennel cough is, however, rather a catch-all term for any cough spreading within a dog population – not just in kennels but also between dogs at a training session or breed show, or even mixing in the park. Many of these infections may not be *B. bronchiseptica* but other viruses, for which one can only treat symptomatically. Parainfluenza virus is often included in a vaccine programme, as it is a common viral cause of kennel cough.

Kennel cough can seem alarming. There is a persistent cough accompanied by production of white, frothy spittle which can last for a matter of weeks, during which time the patient is highly infectious to

Lyme disease is still a relatively rare occurrence in the UK.

other dogs. I remember when it ran through our five Border Collies – there were white patches of froth on the floor wherever you looked! Other features include sneezing, a runny nose and eyes sore with conjunctivitis. Fortunately, these infections are generally self-limiting, most dogs recovering without any long-lasting problems. However, an elderly dog may be knocked sideways by it, akin to the effects of a common cold on a frail elderly person.

LEPTOSPIROSIS

Disease is caused by *Leptospira interogans*, a spiral-shaped bacterium. There are several natural variants or serovars. Each is characteristically found in one or more particular host animal species which then acts as a reservoir, intermittently shedding leptospires in the urine. Infection can also be picked up at mating,

via bite wounds, across the placenta, or through eating the carcases of infected animals (such as rats).

A serovar will cause actual clinical disease in an individual when two conditions are fulfilled: the individual is not the natural host species and is also not immune to that particular serovar.

Leptospirosis is a zoonotic disease, known as Weil's disease in humans, with implications for all those in contact with an affected dog. It is also commonly called rat jaundice, reflecting the rat's important role as a carrier. The UK National Rodent Survey 2003 found a wild brown rat population of 60 million, equivalent at the time to one rat per person. Wherever you live in the UK, rats are endemic, which means that there is as much a risk for the Jack Russell living with a family in a town as the Jack Russell leading a rural lifestyle.

Signs of illness reflect the organs affected by a particular serovar. In humans, there may be a 'flu-like' illness or a more serious, often life-threatening disorder involving major body organs.

The illness in a susceptible dog may be mild, the dog recovering within two to three weeks without treatment but going on to develop long-term liver or kidney disease. In contrast, peracute illness may result in a rapid deterioration and death following initial malaise and fever. There may also be anorexia, vomiting, diarrhoea, abdominal pain, joint pain, increased thirst and rate of urination, jaundice, and ocular changes. Haemorrhage is a common feature because of low platelet numbers, manifesting as bleeding under the skin, nose-bleeds and the presence of blood in the urine and faeces.

Treatment requires rigorous intra-venous fluid therapy to

support the kidneys. Being a bacterial infection, it is possible to treat leptospirosis with specific antibiotics, although a prolonged course of several weeks is needed. Strict hygiene and barrier nursing are required in order to avoid onward transmission of the disease.

Annual vaccination is recommended for leptospirosis, because the immunity only lasts for a year, unlike the longer immunity associated with vaccines against viruses. There is however, little or no cross-protection between Leptospira serovars, so vaccination will result in protection against only those serovars included in the particular vaccine used. Additionally, although vaccination against leptospirosis will prevent active disease if an individual is exposed to a serovar included in the vaccine, it cannot prevent that individual from being infected and becoming a carrier in the long-term.

In the UK, vaccines have classically included L icterohaemorrhagiae (rat-adapted serovar) and L canicola (dog-specific serovar). The latter is of especial significance to us humans, since disease will not be apparent in an infected dog but leptospires will be shed intermittently.

The situation in North America is less clear-cut. Blanket vaccination against leptospirosis is not considered necessary because it only occurs in certain areas. There has also been a shift in the serovars implicated in clinical

LYME DISEASE

This is a bacterial infection transmitted by hard ticks. It is therefore found in those specific areas of the US where ticks are found such as north-eastern states, some southern states, California and the upper Mississippi region. It does also occur in the UK but at a low level so vaccination is not routinely offered.

Clinical disease is manifested primarily as limping due to arthritis, but other organs affected include the heart, kidneys and nervous system. It is readily treatable with appropriate antibiotics, once diagnosed, but the causal bacterium, Borrelia burgdorferi is not cleared from the body totally and will persist.

Prevention requires both vaccination and tick control, especially as there are other diseases transmitted by ticks. Ticks carrying B. burgdorferi will transmit it to humans as well, but an infected dog cannot pass it to a human.

disease, reflecting the effectiveness of vaccination and the migration of wildlife reservoirs carrying different serovars from rural areas, so you must be guided by your veterinarian's knowledge of the local situation.

CANINE PARVOVIRUS (CPV)
Canine Parvovirus disease first appeared in the late 1970's when it was feared that the UK's dog population would be decimated by it because of the lack of immunity in the general canine population. While this was a terrifying possibility at the time, fortunately it did not happen.

There are two forms of the virus (CPV-1, CPV-2) affecting domesticated dogs. It is highly contagious, picked up via the

mouth/nose from infected faeces. The incubation period is about five days.

CPV-2 causes two types of illness: gastro-enteritis and heart disease in puppies born to unvaccinated dams, both of which often result in death.

Infection of puppies less than three weeks of age with CPV-1 manifests as diarrhoea, vomiting, difficulty breathing and fading puppy syndrome. CPV-1 can cause abortion and foetal abnormalities in breeding bitches.

Occurrence is mainly low now, thanks to vaccination, although a recent outbreak in my area did claim the lives of several puppies and dogs. It is also occasionally seen in the elderly unvaccinated dog.

RABIES

This is another zoonotic disease and there are very strict control measures in place. Vaccines were once available in the UK only on an individual basis for dogs being taken abroad. Pets travelling into the UK had to serve six months' compulsory quarantine so that any pet incubating rabies would be identified before release back into the general population. Under the Pet Travel Scheme (PETS), provided certain criteria are met (check the DEFRA website for up-to-date information – www.defra.gov.uk) then dogs can re-enter the UK without being quarantined.

Dogs to be imported into the US have to show that they were vaccinated against rabies at least 30 days previously; otherwise, they have to serve effective internal quarantine for 30 days from the date of vaccination against rabies, in order to ensure they are not incubating the disease. The exception is dogs entering from countries recognised as being rabies-free, in which case it has to be proved that they lived in that country for at least six months beforehand.

PARASITES

A parasite is defined as an organism deriving benefit on a one-way basis from another, the host. It goes without saying that it is not to the parasite's advantage to harm the host to such an extent that the benefit is lost, especially if it results in the death of the host. This means a dog could harbour parasites, internal and/or external, without there being any signs apparent to the owner. Many canine parasites can, however, transfer to humans with variable consequences, so routine preventative treatment is advised against particular parasites.

Just as with vaccination, risk assessment plays a part – for example, there is no need for routine heartworm treatment in the UK (at present), but it is vital in the US and in Mediterranean countries.

ROUNDWORMS (NEMATODES)

These are the spaghetti-like worms which you may have seen passed in faeces or brought up in vomit. Most of the de-worming treatments in use today cause the adults roundworms to disintegrate, thankfully, so that treating puppies in particular is not as unpleasant as it used to be!

Most puppies will have a worm burden, mainly of a particular roundworm species (*Toxocara canis*) which reactivates within the dam's tissues during pregnancy and passes to the foetuses developing in the womb. It is therefore important to treat the dam both during and after pregnancy, as well as the puppies.

Professional advice is to continue worming every one-to-three months. There are roundworm eggs in the environment and unless you examine your dog's faeces under a microscope on a very regular basis for the presence of roundworm eggs, you will be unaware of your dog having picked up roundworms, unless he should have such a heavy burden that he passes the adults.

It takes a few weeks from the time that a dog swallows a *Toxocara canis* roundworm egg to himself passing viable eggs (the pre-patent period). These eggs are not immediately infective to other animals, requiring a period of maturation in the environment which is primarily temperature-dependent and therefore shorter in the summer (as little as two weeks) than in the winter. The eggs can survive in the environment for two years and more.

There are de-worming products which are active all the time, which will provide continuous protection when administered as often as directed. Otherwise, treating every month will, in effect, cut in before a dog could theoretically become a source of roundworm eggs to the general population.

It is the risk to human health which is so important: *T. canis* roundworms will migrate within our tissues and cause all manner of problems, not least of which (but fortunately rarely) is blindness. If a dog has roundworms, the eggs also find their way onto his coat where they can be picked up during stroking. Sensible hygiene is therefore important. You should always carefully pick up your dog's faeces and dispose of them appropriately, thereby preventing the maturation of any eggs present in the fresh faeces.

TAPEWORMS (CESTODES)

When considering the general dog population, the primary source of the commonest tapeworm species will be fleas, which can carry the eggs. Most multi-wormers will be active against these tapeworms. They are not a major threat to human health because human infection is very rare. Nonetheless, it is better to take all reasonable precautions; not least because it is unpleasant to see the wriggly rice grain tapeworm segments emerging from your dog's back passage whilst he is lying in front of the fire, and usually when you have guests for dinner!

A tapeworm of significance to human health is *Echinococcus granulosus*, found in a few parts of the UK, mainly in Wales. Man is an intermediate host for this tapeworm, along with sheep, cattle and pigs. Inadvertent ingestion of eggs passed in the faeces of an infected dog is followed by the development of so-called hydatid cysts in major

The breeder should start a worming programme, which needs to be continued throughout a dog's life.

organs such as the lungs and liver, necessitating surgical removal. Dogs become infected through eating raw meat containing hydatid cysts. Cooking will kill hydatid cysts, so avoid feeding raw meat and offal in areas of high risk.

There are specific requirements for treatment with praziquantel within 24 to 48 hours of return into the UK under the PETS. This is to prevent the introduction of *Echinococcus multilocularis*, a tapeworm carried by foxes on mainland Europe which is transmissible to humans, causing serious or even fatal liver disease.

HEARTWORM (DIROFILARIA IMMITIS)

Heartworm infection has been diagnosed in dogs all over the world. There are two

prerequisites: presence of mosquitoes and a warm humid climate.

When a female mosquito bites an infected animal, it acquires *D. immitis* in its circulating form, as microfilariae. A warm environmental temperature is needed for these microfilariae to develop into the infective third-stage larvae (L3) within the mosquitoes, the so-called intermediate host. L3 larvae are then transmitted by the mosquito when it next bites a dog. Therefore, while heartworm infection is found in all the states of the US, it is at differing levels. An occurrence in Alaska, for example, is probably a reflection of a visiting dog having previously picked up the infection elsewhere.

Heartworm infection is not

currently a problem in the UK, except for those dogs contracting it while abroad without suitable preventative treatment. Global warming and its effect on the UK's climate, however, could change that.

It is a potentially life-threatening condition, with dogs of all breeds and ages being susceptible without preventative treatment. The larvae can grow to 14 inches within the right side of the heart, causing primarily signs of heart failure and ultimately liver and kidney damage. It can be treated, but prevention is a better plan. In the US, regular blood tests for the presence of infection are advised, coupled with appropriate preventative measures, so I would advise liaison with your veterinary surgeon.

For dogs travelling to heartworm-endemic areas of the EU such as the Mediterranean coast, preventative treatment should be started before leaving the UK and maintained during the visit. Again, this is best arranged with your veterinary surgeon.

FLEAS

There are several species of flea, which are not host-specific. A dog can be carrying cat and human fleas as well as dog fleas, but the same flea treatment will

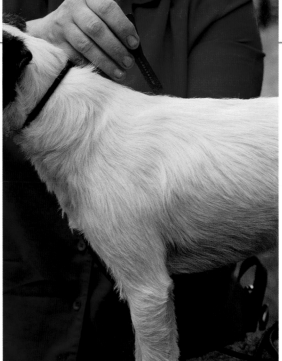

Spot on treatment is an effective method of preventing flea infestation.

kill and/or control them all. It is also accepted that environmental control is a vital part of a flea control programme. This is because the adult flea is only on the animal for as long as it takes to have a blood meal and to breed; the remainder of the life cycle occurs in the house, car, caravan, shed …

There is a vast array of flea control products available, with various routes of administration: collar, powder, spray, 'spot-on', oral. Flea control needs to be applied to all pets in the house, regardless of whether they leave the house, since fleas can be introduced into the house by other pets and their human owners. Discuss your specific flea control needs with your vet.

MITES

There are five types of mite which can affect dogs:

(i) Demodex canis: This is a normal inhabitant of canine hair follicles, passed from the bitch to her pups as they suckle. The development of actual skin disease or demodicosis depends on the individual. It is seen frequently around the time of puberty and after a bitch's first season, associated with hormonal changes. There may, however, be an inherited weakness in an individual's immune system enabling multiplication of the mite.

The localised form consists of areas of fur loss without itchiness, generally around the face and on the forelimbs, and 90 per cent will recover without treatment. The other 10 per cent develop the juvenile-onset generalised form, of which half will recover spontaneously. The other half may be depressed, go off their food and show signs of itchiness due to secondary bacterial skin infections.

Treatment may be prolonged over several months and consists of regular bathing with a specific miticidal shampoo, often clipping away fur to improve access to the skin, together with a suitable antibiotic by mouth. There is also now a licensed 'spot-on' preparation available. Progress is monitored by examination of deep skin scrapings for the presence of the mite; the initial diagnosis is based upon abnormally high numbers of the mite, often with live individuals being seen.

Some Jack Russells may develop the generalised form of demodicosis for the first time in middle-age (more than about four years of age). This often reflects underlying immunosuppression by an internal disease so it is important to identify such a cause and correct it where possible, as well as specifically treating the skin condition.

(ii) Sarcoptes scabei: This characteristically causes an intense pruritus or itchiness in the affected Jack Russell, causing him to incessantly scratch and bite at himself, leading to marked fur loss and skin trauma. Initially starting on the elbows, ear flaps and hocks, without treatment the skin on the rest of the body can become involved, with thickening and pigmentation of the skin. Secondary bacterial infections are common.

Unlike Demodex, this mite lives at the skin surface and it can be hard to find in skin scrapings. It is therefore not unusual to treat a patient for sarcoptic mange (scabies) based on the appearance of the problem even with negative skin scraping findings, and especially if there is a history of contact with foxes which are a frequent source of

Skin problems can occur for the first time in middle age.

the scabies mite.

It will spread between dogs and can therefore also be found in situations where large numbers of dogs from different backgrounds are mixing together. It will cause itchiness in humans, although the mite cannot complete its life cycle on us, so treating all affected dogs should be sufficient. Fortunately, there is now a highly effective 'spot-on' treatment for *Sarcoptes scabei*.

(iii) Cheyletiella yasguri: This is the fur mite most commonly

found on dogs. It is often called 'walking dandruff' because it can be possible to see collections of the small white mite moving about over the skin surface. There is excessive scale and dandruff formation and mild itchiness. It is transmissible to humans, causing a pruritic rash. Diagnosis is by microscopic examination of skin scrapings, coat combings and sticky tape impressions from the skin and fur. Treatment is with an appropriate insecticide, as advised by your veterinary surgeon.

TICKS

Ticks have become an increasing problem in recent years throughout Britain. Their physical presence causes irritation, but it is their potential to spread disease that causes concern. A tick will transmit any infection previously contracted while feeding on an animal: for example Borrelia burgdorferi, the causal agent of Lyme disease (see page 135).

The life cycle is curious: each life stage takes a year to develop and move on to the next. Long grass is a major habitat. The vibration of animals moving through the grass will stimulate the larva, nymph or adult to climb up a blade of grass and wave its legs in the air as it 'quests' for a host on to which to latch for its next blood meal. Humans are as likely to be hosts, so ramblers and orienteers are advised to cover their legs when going through rough long grass.

Removing a tick is simple – provided your dog will stay still. The important rule is to twist gently so that the tick is persuaded to let go with its mouthparts. Grasp the body of the tick as near to your dog's skin as possible, either between thumb and fingers or with a specific tick-removing instrument, and then rotate in one direction until the tick comes away. I keep a plastic tick hook in my wallet at all times.

(iv) Otodectes cynotis: A highly transmissible otitis externa (outer ear infection) results from the presence in the outer ear canal of this ear mite, characterised by exuberant production of dark earwax. The patient will frequently shake his head and rub at the ear(s) affected. The mites can also spread on to the skin adjacent to the opening of the external ear canal and may transfer elsewhere such as to the paws.

When using an otoscope to examine the outer ear canal, the heat from the light source will often cause any ear mites present to start moving around. I often offer owners the chance to have a look because it really is quite an extraordinary sight! It is also possible to identify the mite from earwax smeared onto a slide and examined under a microscope.

Cats are a common source of ear mites. It is not unusual to find ear mites during the routine examination of puppies and kittens. Treatment options include specific ear drops acting against both the mite and any secondary infections present in the auditory canal, and certain 'spot-on' formulations. It is vital to treat all dogs and cats in the household to prevent recycling of the mite between individuals.

(v) The free-living mite (Neo-) Trombicula autumnalis or harvest mite: This can cause an intense local irritation on the skin. Its larvae are picked up from undergrowth, so they are characteristically found as a bright orange patch on the web of skin between the digits of the paws. It feeds on skin cells before dropping off to complete its life cycle in the environment.

Its name is a little misleading, because it is not restricted to the autumn nor to harvest-time; I find it on the ear flaps of cats from late June onwards, depending on the prevailing weather. It will also bite humans.

Treatment depends on identifying and avoiding hotspots for picking up harvest mites, if possible. Checking the skin, especially the paws, after exercise and mechanically removing any mites found will reduce the chances of irritation, which can be treated symptomatically. Insecticides can also be applied – be guided by your veterinary surgeon.

A-Z OF COMMON AILMENTS

ANAL SACS, IMPACTED
The anal sacs lie on either side of the back passage or anus at approximately four- and eight-o'-clock, if compared with the face of a clock. They fill with a particularly pungent fluid which is emptied onto the faeces as they

move past the sacs to exit from the anus. Theories abound as to why these sacs should become impacted periodically and seemingly more so in some dogs than others.

The irritation of impacted anal sacs is often seen as 'scooting', when the backside is dragged along the ground. Some dogs will gnaw at their back feet or over the rump.

Increasing the fibre content of the diet helps some dogs; in others, there is underlying skin disease. It may be a one-off occurrence for no apparent reason. Sometimes, an infection can become established, requiring antibiotic therapy which may need to be coupled with flushing out the infected sac under sedation or general anaesthesia. More rarely, a dog will present with an apparently acute-onset anal sac abscess which is incredibly painful.

Check your Jack Russell's ears regularly to ensure they are clean and free from infection, foreign bodies, or ear mites.

DIARRHOEA
Cause and treatment much as Gastritis (see below).

EAR INFECTIONS
The dog has a long external ear canal, initially vertical then horizontal, leading to the eardrum which protects the middle ear. If your Jack Russell is shaking his head, then his ears will need to be inspected with an auroscope by a veterinary surgeon in order to identify any cause, and to ensure the eardrum is intact. A sample may be taken from the canal to be examined under the microscope and cultured to identify causal agents before prescribing appropriate ear drops containing antibiotic, anti-fungal agent and/or steroid. Predisposing causes of otitis externa or infection in the external ear canal include: presence of a foreign body such as a grass awn; ear mites, which are intensely irritating to the dog and stimulate the production of brown wax, predisposing to infection; previous infections causing the canal's lining to thicken, narrowing the canal and reducing ventilation; swimming – some Jack Russells love swimming, but water trapped in the external ear canal can lead to infection, especially if the water is not clean.

FOREIGN BODIES
Internal: Items swallowed in haste without checking whether they will be digested, can cause problems if they lodge in the stomach or obstruct the intestines, necessitating surgical removal. Acute vomiting is the main sign. Common objects I have seen removed include stones from the garden, peach stones, babies' dummies, golf

This is an exceptionally agile breed – but joint problems can develop.

balls and, once, a lady's bra …

It is possible to diagnose a dog with an intestinal obstruction across a waiting room from a particularly 'tucked-up' stance and pained facial expression. These patients bounce back from surgery dramatically. A previously docile and compliant obstructed patient will return for a post-operative check-up and literally bounce into the consulting room.

External: Grass awns are adept at finding their way into orifices such as a nostril, down an ear,

and into the soft skin between two digits (toes), whence they start a one-way journey due to the direction of their whiskers. In particular, I remember a grass awn which migrated from a hind paw, causing abscesses along the way but not yielding itself up until it erupted through the skin in the groin!

GASTRITIS

This is usually a simple stomach upset, most commonly in response to dietary indiscretion. Scavenging constitutes a change in the diet as much as an abrupt

switch in the food being fed by the owner.

There are also some specific infections causing more severe gastritis/enteritis which will require treatment from a veterinary surgeon (See also Canine Parvovirus under 'Vaccination' earlier).

Generally, a day without food followed by a few days of small, frequent meals of a bland diet (such as cooked chicken or fish), or an appropriate prescription diet, should allow the stomach to settle. It is vital to ensure the patient is drinking and retaining sufficient to cover losses resulting from the stomach upset in addition to the normal losses to be expected when healthy. Oral rehydration fluid may not be very appetising for the patient, in which case cooled boiled water should be offered. Fluids should initially be offered in small but frequent amounts to avoid over-drinking, which can result in further vomiting and thereby dehydration and electrolyte imbalances.

It is also important to gradually wean the patient back on to routine food or else another bout of gastritis may occur.

JOINT PROBLEMS

It is not unusual for older Jack Russells to be stiff after exercise, particularly in cold weather. This is not really surprising, given that they are such busy dogs when young, rushing around in hedgerows and ditches. This is such a game breed that a nine or ten year old Jack Russell will not readily forego an extra walk, or take kindly to turning for home earlier than usual. Your veterinary surgeon will be able to advise you on ways for helping your dog cope with stiffness, not least of which will be to ensure that he is not overweight. Arthritic joints do not need to be burdened with extra bodyweight!

LUMPS

Regularly handling and stroking your dog will enable the early detection of lumps and bumps. These may be due to infection (abscess), bruising, multiplication of particular cells from within the body, or even an external parasite (tick). If you are worried about any lump you find, have it checked by a veterinary surgeon.

OBESITY

Being overweight does predispose to many other problems such as diabetes mellitus, heart disease and joint problems. It is so easily prevented by simply acting as your Jack Russell's conscience. Ignore pleading eyes and feed according to your dog's waistline. The body condition is what matters qualitatively, alongside monitoring that individual's bodyweight as a quantitative measure. The Jack Russell should, in my opinion as a health professional, have at least a suggestion of a waist and it should be possible to feel the ribs beneath only a slight layer of fat.

Neutering does not automatically mean that your Jack Russell will be overweight. Having an ovario-hysterectomy

does slow down the body's rate of working, castration to a lesser extent, but it therefore means that your dog needs less food. I recommend cutting back a little on the amount of food fed a few weeks before neutering to accustom your Jack Russell to less food. If she looks a little underweight on the morning of the operation, it will help the veterinary surgeon as well as giving her a little leeway weight-wise afterwards.

It is always harder to lose weight after neutering than before, because of this slowing in the body's inherent metabolic rate.

TEETH

Eating food starts with the canine teeth gripping and killing prey in the wild, incisor teeth biting off pieces of food and the molar teeth chewing it. To be able to eat is vital for life, yet the actual health of the teeth is often over-looked: unhealthy teeth can predispose to disease, and not just by reducing the ability to eat. The presence of infection within the mouth can lead to bacteria entering the bloodstream and then filtering out at major organs, with the potential for serious consequences. That is not to forget that simply having dental pain can affect a dog's well being, as anyone who has had toothache will confirm.

Veterinary dentistry has made huge leaps in recent years, so that it no longer consists of extraction as the treatment of necessity.

Good dental health lies in the

Feeding the correct diet will promote dental health.

hands of the owner, starting from the moment the dog comes into your care. Just as we have taken on responsibility for feeding, so we have acquired the task of maintaining good dental and oral hygiene. In an ideal world, we should brush our dogs' teeth as regularly as our own, but the Jack Russell puppy who finds having his teeth brushed is a huge game and excuse to roll over and over on the ground, requires loads of patience, twice a day.

There are alternative strategies ranging from dental chew-sticks to specially formulated foods, but the main thing is to be aware of your dog's mouth. At least train your puppy to permit full examination of his teeth, which will not only ensure you are checking in his mouth regularly but also make your veterinary surgeon's job easier when there is a real need for your dog to 'Open wide!'

Fortunately the Parson Russell Terrier (above) and the Jack Russell are relatively free from inherited disorders.

INHERITED DISORDERS

Any individual, dog or human, may have an inherited disorder by virtue of genes acquired from the parents. This is significant not only for the health of that individual, but also because of the potential for transmitting the disorder on to that individual's offspring and to subsequent generations, depending on the mode of inheritance.

There are control schemes in place for some inherited disorders. In the US, for example, the Canine Eye Registration Foundation (CERF) was set up by dog breeders concerned about heritable eye disease and provides a database of dogs who have been examined by diplomates of the American College of Veterinary Ophthalmologists.

Few inherited conditions have been confirmed in the Jack and Parson Russell Terriers. The most significant is Primary lens luxation. There is an autosomal dominant pattern of inheritance to this condition, whereby the lens slips from its usual position within the eye. It tends to occur in the young adult onwards and can result in blindness unless detected and treated early on. This is controlled under Schedule A of the BVA/KC/ISDS (British Veterinary Association/Kennel Club/International Sheepdog Society) Scheme in the UK, CERF in the US.

Other conditions documented in the Jack Russell include Legg-Calve-Perthes disease, patellar luxation, glaucoma and deafness.

COMPLEMENTARY THERAPIES

Just as for human health, I do believe there is a place for alternative therapies, but alongside and complementing orthodox treatment under the supervision of a veterinary surgeon. That is why 'complementary therapies' is a better name.

Because animals do not have a choice, there are measures in place to safeguard their wellbeing and welfare. All manipulative treatment must be under the direction of a veterinary surgeon who has examined the patient and diagnosed the condition which she or he feels needs that form of treatment. This covers physiotherapy, chiropractic, osteopathy and swimming therapy. For example, dogs with arthritis who cannot exercise as freely as they were accustomed, will enjoy the sensation of controlled non-weight-bearing exercise in water and benefit with improved muscling and overall fitness.

All other complementary

therapies, such as acupuncture, homeopathy and aromatherapy, can only be carried out by veterinary surgeons who have been trained in that particular field. Acupuncture is mainly used in dogs for pain relief, often to good effect. The needles look more alarming to the owner, but they are very fine and are well tolerated by most canine patients. Speaking personally, superficial needling is not unpleasant and does help with pain relief. Homeopathy has had a mixed press in recent years. It is based on the concept of treating like with like. Additionally, a homeopathic remedy is said to become more powerful the more it is diluted.

SUMMARY

As the owner of a Jack Russell, you are responsible for his care and health. Not only must you make decisions on his behalf, you are also responsible for establishing a life-style for him which will ensure he leads a long and happy life. Diet plays as important a part in this as exercise, for example.

For the domestic dog, it is only in recent years that the need has been recognised for changing the diet to suit the dog as he grows, matures and then enters his twilight years. So-called life-stage diets try to match the nutritional needs of the dog as he progresses through life.

An adult dog food will suit the Jack Russell living a standard family life. There are also foods for those Jack Russells tactfully

With good care and management, you should enjoy many years of happy companionship.

termed as obese-prone, such as those who have been neutered or are less active than others, or simply like their food. Do remember though, that ultimately you are in control of your Jack Russell's diet, unless he is able to profit from scavenging!

On the other hand, prescription diets are of necessity fed under the supervision of a veterinary surgeon because each is formulated to meet the very specific needs of a particular health condition. Should a

prescription diet be fed to a healthy dog, or to a dog with a different illness, there could be adverse effects.

It is important to remember that your Jack Russell has no choice. As his owner, you are responsible for any decision made, so it must be as informed a decision as possible. Always speak to your veterinary surgeon if you have any worries about your Jack Russell. He is not just a dog: from the moment you brought him home, he became a member of the family.

THE AUTHORS

EMILY BATES

Emily Bates has been involved with dogs for well over thirty years, during which time she has exhibited show dogs with considerable success. Also a caring breeder and Championship Show judge, she awards Challenge Certificates in four breeds, with others on the near horizon. She judges extensively abroad where her expertise, and also her lectures on dogs, are in high demand.

Greatly interested in all breeds, with a particular penchant for canine history, Emily Bates has written a number of dog books, several of which have been translated into other languages. She also writes regularly for the dog press, both in the UK and overseas.

JULIA BARNES

Julia has owned and trained a number of different dog breeds, and is a puppy socialiser for Dogs for the Disabled. A former journalist, she has written many books, including several on dog training and behaviour.
See Chapter Six: Training and Socialisation.

ALISON LOGAN MA VetMB MRCVS

Alison qualified as a veterinary surgeon from Cambridge University in 1989, having been brought up surrounded by all manner of animals and birds in the north Essex countryside. She has been in practice in her home town ever since, living with her husband, two children and Labrador Retriever Pippin.

She contributes on a regular basis to *Veterinary Times, Veterinary Nurse Times, Dogs Today, Cat World* and *Pet Patter*, the PetPlan newsletter. In 1995, Alison won the Univet Literary Award with an article on Cushing's Disease, and she won it again (as the Vetoquinol Literary Award) in 2002, writing about common conditions in the Shar-Pei.
See Chapter Eight: Happy and Healthy.

USEFUL ADDRESSES

KENNEL & BREED CLUBS

UK
The Kennel Club
1 Clarges Street, London, W1J 8AB
Tel: 0870 606 6750
Fax: 0207 518 1058
Web: www.the-kennel-club.org.uk

To obtain up-to-date contact information for the following breed clubs, contact the Kennel Club:
• Jack Russell Club of Great Britain
• Jack Russell Club of East Anglia
• Jack Russell Terrier UK
• Parson Russell Terrier Club

USA
American Kennel Club (AKC)
5580 Centerview Drive,
Raleigh, NC 27606, USA.
Tel: 919 233 9767
Fax: 919 233 3627
Email: info@akc.org
Web: www.akc.org

United Kennel Club (UKC)
100 E Kilgore Rd, Kalamazoo,
MI 49002-5584, USA.
Tel: 269 343 9020
Fax: 269 343 7037
Web:www.ukcdogs.com/

The Jack Russell Terrier Club of America, Inc.
Web: http://www.therealjackrussell.com/

For contact details of regional clubs, please contact
The Jack Russell Terrier Club of America.

AUSTRALIA
Australian National Kennel Council (ANKC)
The Australian National Kennel Council is the administrative body for pure breed canine affairs in Australia. It does not, however, deal directly with dog exhibitors, breeders or judges. For information pertaining to breeders, clubs or shows, please contact the relevant State or Territory Controlling Body.

Dogs Australian Capital Teritory
PO Box 815, Dickson ACT 2602
Tel: (02) 6241 4404
Fax: (02) 6241 1129
Email: administrator@dogsact.org.au
Web: www.dogsact.org.au

Dogs New South Wales
PO Box 632, St Marys, NSW 1790
Tel: (02) 9834 3022 or 1300 728 022 (NSW Only)
Fax: (02) 9834 3872
Email: info@dogsnsw.org.au
Web: www.dogsnsw.org.au

Dogs Northern Territory
PO Box 37521, Winnellie NT 0821

Tel: (08) 8984 3570
Fax: (08) 8984 3409
Email: admin@dogsnt.com.au
Web: www.dogsnt.com.au

Dogs Queensland
PO Box 495, Fortitude Valley Qld 4006
Tel: (07) 3252 2661
Fax: (07) 3252 3864
Email: info@dogsqueensland.org.au
Web: www.dogsqueensland.org.au

Dogs South Australia
PO Box 844
Prospect East SA 5082
Tel: (08) 8349 4797
Fax: (08) 8262 5751
Email: info@dogssa.com.au
Web: www.dogssa.com.au

Tasmanian Canine Association Inc
The Rothman Building
PO Box 116
Glenorchy Tas 7010
Tel: (03) 6272 9443
Fax: (03) 6273 0844
Email: tca@iprimus.com.au
Web: www.tasdogs.com

Dogs Victoria
Locked Bag K9
Cranbourne VIC 3977
Tel: (03)9788 2500
Fax: (03) 9788 2599
Email: office@dogsvictoria.org.au
Web: www.dogsvictoria.org.au

Dogs Western Australia
PO Box 1404
Canning Vale WA 6970
Tel: (08) 9455 1188
Fax: (08) 9455 1190
Email: k9@dogswest.com
Web: www.dogswest.com

INTERNATIONAL
Fédération Cynologique Internationalé (FCI)/World Canine Organisation
Place Albert 1er, 13, B-6530 Thuin,
Belgium.
Tel: +32 71 59.12.38
Fax: +32 71 59.22.29
Web: www.fci.be/

TRAINING AND BEHAVIOUR

UK
Association of Pet Dog Trainers
PO Box 17, Kempsford, GL7 4WZ
Telephone: 01285 810811
Email: APDToffice@aol.com
Web: http://www.apdt.co.uk

Association of Pet Behaviour Counsellors
PO BOX 46, Worcester, WR8 9YS
Telephone: 01386 751151
Fax: 01386 750743
Email: info@apbc.org.uk
Web: http://www.apbc.org.uk/

USA
Association of Pet Dog Trainers
101 North Main Street, Suite 610
Greenville, SC 29601, USA.
Tel: 1 800 738 3647
Email: information@apdt.com
Web: www.apdt.com/

American College of Veterinary Behaviorists
College of Veterinary Medicine, 4474 Tamu, Texas
A&M University
College Station, Texas 77843-4474
Web: http://dacvb.org/

American Veterinary Society of Animal Behavior
Web: www.avsabonline.org/

AUSTRALIA
APDT Australia Inc
PO Box 3122, Bankstown Square, NSW 2200,
Email: secretary@apdt.com.au
Web: www.apdt.com.au

Canine Behaviour
For details of regional behvaiourists, contact the relevant State or Territory Controlling Body.

ACTIVITIES

UK
Agility Club
http://www.agilityclub.co.uk/

British Flyball Association
PO Box 990, Doncaster, DN1 9FY
Telephone: 01628 829623
Email: secretary@flyball.org.uk
Web: http://www.flyball.org.uk/

USA
North American Dog Agility Council
P.O. Box 1206, Colbert,
OK 74733, USA.
Web: www.nadac.com/

North American Flyball Association, Inc.
1333 West Devon Avenue, #512
Chicago, IL 60660
Tel/Fax: 800 318 6312
Email: flyball@flyball.org
Web: www.flyball.org/

AUSTRALIA
Agility Dog Association of Australia
ADAA Secretary, PO Box 2212,
Gailes, QLD 4300, Australia.
Tel: 0423 138 914

Email: admin@adaa.com.au
Web: www.adaa.com.au/

NADAC Australia (North American Dog Agility Council - Australian Division)
12 Wellman Street, Box Hill South, Victoria 3128, Australia.
Email: shirlene@nadacaustralia.com
Web: www.nadacaustralia.com/

Australian Flyball Association
PO Box 4179, Pitt Town, NSW 2756
Tel: 0407 337 939
Email: info@flyball.org.au
Web: www.flyball.org.au/

INTERNATIONAL

World Canine Freestyle Organisation
P.O. Box 350122, Brooklyn, NY 11235-2525, USA
Tel: (718) 332-8336
Fax: (718) 646-2686
Email: wcfodogs@aol.com
Web: www.worldcaninefreestyle.org

HEALTH

UK

Alternative Veterinary Medicine Centre
Chinham House, Stanford in the Vale, Oxfordshire, SN7 8NQ
Tel: 01367 710324
Fax: 01367 718243
Web: www.alternativevet.org/

British Small Animal Veterinary Association
Woodrow House, 1 Telford Way, Waterwells Business Park, Quedgeley, Gloucestershire, GL2 2AB
Tel: 01452 726700
Fax: 01452 726701
Email: customerservices@bsava.com
Web: http://www.bsava.com/

Royal College of Veterinary Surgeons
Belgravia House, 62-64 Horseferry Road, London, SW1P 2AF
Tel: 0207 222 2001
Fax: 0207 222 2004
Email: admin@rcvs.org.uk
Web: www.rcvs.org.uk

USA

American Holistic Veterinary Medical Association
2218 Old Emmorton Road
Bel Air, MD 21015
Tel: 410 569 0795
Fax 410 569 2346
Email: office@ahvma.org
Web: www.ahvma.org/

American Veterinary Medical Association
1931 North Meacham Road, Suite 100, Schaumburg, IL 60173-4360, USA.
Tel: 800 248 2862
Fax: 847 925 1329
Web: www.avma.org

American College of Veterinary Surgeons
19785 Crystal Rock Dr, Suite 305
Germantown, MD 20874, USA.
Tel: 301 916 0200
Toll Free: 877 217 2287
Fax: 301 916 2287
Email: acvs@acvs.org
Web: www.acvs.org/

AUSTRALIA
Australian Holistic Vets
Web: www.ahv.com.au/

Australian Small Animal Veterinary Association
40/6 Herbert Street, St Leonards, NSW 2065, Australia.
Tel: 02 9431 5090
Fax: 02 9437 9068
Email: asava@ava.com.au
Web: www.asava.com.au

Australian Veterinary Association
Unit 40, 6 Herbert Street, St Leonards, NSW 2065, Australia.
Tel: 02 9431 5000
Fax: 02 9437 9068
Web: www.ava.com.au

Australian College Veterinary Scientists
Building 3, Garden City Office Park, 2404 Logan Road, Eight Mile Plains, Queensland 4113, Australia.
Tel: 07 3423 2016
Fax: 07 3423 2977
Email: admin@acvs.org.au
Web: http://acvsc.org.au

ASSISTANCE DOGS

UK
Canine Partners
Mill Lane, Heyshott, Midhurst, GU29 0ED
Tel: 08456 580480
Fax: 08456 580481
Web: www.caninepartners.co.uk

Dogs for the Disabled
The Frances Hay Centre, Blacklocks Hill, Banbury, Oxon, OX17 2BS
Tel: 01295 252600
Web: www.dogsforthedisabled.org

Guide Dogs for the Blind Association
Burghfield Common, Reading, RG7 3YG
Tel: 01189 835555

Fax: 01189 835433
Web: www.guidedogs.org.uk/

Hearing Dogs for Deaf People
The Grange, Wycombe Road, Saunderton, Princes Risborough, Bucks, HP27 9NS
Tel: 01844 348100
Fax: 01844 348101
Web: www.hearingdogs.org.uk

Pets as Therapy
14a High Street, Wendover, Aylesbury, Bucks. HP22 6EA.
Tel: 01845 345445
Fax: 01845 550236
Web: http://www.petsastherapy.org/

Support Dogs
21 Jessops Riverside, Brightside Lane, Sheffield, S9 2RX
Tel: 01142 617800
Fax: 01142 617555
Email: supportdogs@btconnect.com
Web: www.support-dogs.org.uk

USA
Therapy Dogs International
88 Bartley Road, Flanders, NJ 07836,.
Tel: 973 252 9800
Fax: 973 252 7171
Web: www.tdi-dog.o

Therapy Dogs Inc.
P.O. Box 20227, Cheyenne, WY 82003.
Tel: 307 432 0272.
Fax: 307-638-2079
Web: www.therapydogs.com

Delta Society - Pet Partners
875 124th Ave NE, Suite 101, Bellevue, WA 98005 USA.
Email: info@DeltaSociety.org
Web: www.deltasociety.org

Comfort Caring Canines
8135 Lare Street, Philadelphia, PA 19128.
Email: ccc@comfortcaringcanines.org
Web: www.comfortcaringcanines.org/

AUSTRALIA
AWARE Dogs Australia, Inc
PO Box 883, Kuranda, Queensland, 488..
Tel: 07 4093 8152
Web: www.awaredogs.org.au/

Delta Society — Therapy Dogs
Web: www.deltasociety.com.au